The Light House

Collection of Motivational Stories…

MAGADA

BlueRose ONE
Stories Matter
NewDelhi • London

BLUEROSE PUBLISHERS
India | U.K.

BlueRose ONE
Stories Matter
New Delhi • London

For permissions requests or inquiries regarding this publication, please contact:

BLUEROSE PUBLISHERS
www.BlueRoseONE.com
info@bluerosepublishers.com
+91 8882 898 898
+4407342408967

ISBN: 978-93-7310-392-1

First Edition: September 2025

"

Dedicated to my wife Rekha, son Reshi Magada,
my source of inspiration 'Gangamma' —my mother
and all my Fishcos[1]

"

[1] All the alumni from the College of Fisheries, Mangalore, India are collectively known as 'Fishcos'

Abnormal Distribution of My Thoughts...

Some stories are retold endlessly — woven into poems, echoed in novels, or brought to life on screens through serials and films. They often revolve around heartbreak, separation, and unfulfilled longing. Over time, we've come to believe that only those stories filled with pain and tragedy are worthy of being called "great" love stories.

As a matter of fact, my love story is one of the greatest love stories. It has happened and still continuing. The world may never recognize it, but it needs no validation, for its greatness speaks for itself between me and my love (Rekha). It does not conform to any formula or framework laid down by the world. No definition, theory, or standard measure can contain it. What I experience exists beyond conventions and calculations—it flows in its own way, unbound, untouched, and incomparable.

But life, much like mathematics, is not limited to a single formula. While drama may dominate centre stage, there are countless quieter equations being solved all around us — subtle interactions, unspoken bonds, and moments of affection that leave no trace in history books or film reels, yet define the very core of human existence.

These unsung stories unfold in everyday life. Love that doesn't scream, but whispers. It grows in the tender glance between a flower vendor and a regular buyer, in the nod of respect between a student and a teacher, or in the silent companionship of two strangers sharing a train seat. It lives in early morning walks, in quiet libraries, in the loyalty of a pet, and in the wordless comfort between siblings.

At times, it deepens between spouses over the years. At other times, it blooms for a moment, then disappears — leaving behind only warmth. Occasionally, it even transcends species — a soulful, silent bond between a human and an animal. These equations may differ in shape and structure, but the mathematical formula of life remains constant: connection, emotion, and meaning.

It was during one of my quiet reflections that a realization anchored itself within me — one that defines this collection:

"There is only one kind of love in this world; Intensity and Purpose may vary."

Love, like a universal constant, exists in every life. What changes is how deeply it is felt and for what reason it appears. Sometimes it comes with purpose, sometimes with no explanation at all. Sometimes it's fleeting, sometimes forever. But the '*X*' in this life's formula — the unknown — is where we find its truest power. I've deliberately wanted to title this book as 'Cont + X' to symbolize both the 'unknown' and the act of 'erasing' in computer language. At times, we unknowingly delete certain moments or emotions from our memory — not because they lack meaning, but because life moves forward and rewrites over them. Later, I changed it to "The Light House," because the light also quite absurd with its vibrancy and frequency. Though it can be studied with advance science tools, still it is an absurd for the normal people. In the endless of light, whether you 'catch the ray of light' or 'catch the entire light' or 'dissolve in it' depends on you and your purpose.

This book is a modest collection of stories — some lived, some heard, some imagined, and others whispered from the quiet corners of the heart. In the first seven chapters, I attempt to unravel the subtle formulas of life; thereafter, the focus shifts to a thoughtful philosophical lens. These stories invite you to explore life from different perspectives and beyond. The small absurdities they hold are not grand, but rather simple, heartfelt moments where love emerges in its purest form — often unnoticed, yet profoundly real.

My hope is that in these pages, you'll begin to see the mathematics of your own life: the constants you rely on, the variables that challenge you, and the quiet moments of symmetry that offer meaning. May these stories inspire you to recognize the beauty in your own journey, love more freely, and embrace the unseen forces that shape your every day.

We may not live for 150 years. But we do have — this moment, this heartbeat, this breath. Let us live it fully. Let us love without any expectations, without any conditions — purely and wholeheartedly. Because love, when true, finds its way back. Often, with a value greater than what we ever imagined.

Although I always had plans to publish my books, I never set a specific timeframe for it. Then, one fine day, Mr. Adithya and Mr. Karthik from Blue Rose Publications reached out to me. Their polite approach and consistent follow-up left me with no room to refuse. The book ultimately saw the light of day purely because of their persistence and unwavering support.

I have used one of the paintings available on Google and extend my heartfelt gratitude to its original creator for his/her work. The entire profit may be given to the artiste. This book is created with no intention of profit. Let us join hands to spread the light of love across the world.

With lots of love—

Dr Shivakumar **Magada**
Mangalore, India
shivakumarmagada@gmail.com

Contents

Foreword…

You Write it, after Reading this Book.

"The fear in thought cuts deeper than reality itself—Magada"

$\pi r^2 h$

The Geometry of Life: A Reflection through the Cylinder

This is a mathematical formula used for the calculation of the volume of a cylinder:

Volume=$\pi r^2 h$

At first glance, it seems like a simple equation — a logical structure to measure space. But beneath the precision of this mathematical truth lies a profound metaphor for life itself.

Our existence, too, begins with a circle — a closed, simple, and perfect form. That circle could be seen as our birth, our origin, our core identity. Its diameter, a straight line passing through the centre, represents the connection between our past and future. And yet, to grasp the full scope of this circle — its circumference — we must walk a journey approximately 3.14 times the length of that straight path. That number, π (pi), is irrational, endless, unknowable in its entirety — much like the unpredictable, infinite nature of life.

As time passes, circles stack upon circles, like the annual rings of a tree, and our once-flat existence gains depth. We grow. We learn. We rise. And just like that, a cylinder begins to form — a structure of experience, memory, growth, and dimension. Height is added to our being, and with it, weight and presence. We move from mere existence to volume — the space we occupy not just physically, but emotionally, spiritually, and ethically.

And here's the beauty: no matter how big or small the circle, no matter how tall the cylinder becomes, the formula remains unchanged. The truth embedded in its structure is constant. In the same way, the essence of life — its need for connection, growth, and meaning — does not vary based on one's background, culture, religion, or region. We are all cylinders in motion — shaped by time, grounded in origin, defined not just by the base we started from, but by the height we build through our actions, choices, and purpose.

The cylinder teaches us that while our radius (our circumstances) may differ, and our height (our life's span or achievement) may vary, what gives us volume — what makes us whole — is consistent across all. It is the elegant fusion of what we are born into and what we choose to become.

The story begins here...

There was a remarkable young woman named Hema — graceful, intelligent, and brimming with promise. Her brilliance in mathematics set her apart early on, and her dedication earned her a coveted seat at the prestigious National Institute of Technology, Karnataka (NITK), Suratkal, one of India's finest engineering institutions. She had secured her place entirely on merit, a testament to her unwavering focus and academic excellence.

Hema chose to pursue Computer Science, a field that excited her with its endless possibilities and power to shape the future. The day she stepped onto the NITK campus, she was filled with a sense of pride and joy — not just for the milestone she had achieved, but for the life she was about to build.

More than just academics, Hema was driven by an inner fire — a desire to live fully, courageously, and unapologetically. She dreamed not only of solving complex algorithms but also of embracing life in all its colours. She wanted to see the world, meet people from different walks of life, and immerse herself in cultures far and wide. Above all, she was determined to prove to the world — and to herself — that she was capable of carving her own path. Independent and spirited, she envisioned a life where she was free to explore, to travel, to create, and to celebrate the journey of becoming the woman she aspired to be.

She met Raghavendra Pai at the 'Ashwa Club' — a collaborative club focused on the exploration of the Internet of Things (IoT) in the design and development of innovative gadgets aimed at solving everyday problems. The club's core mission was to integrate Artificial Intelligence (AI) into these smart systems, enabling the devices not only to function efficiently but also to learn, adapt, and respond intelligently to user needs and environmental conditions.

Raghavendra Pai was, in every academic sense, a prodigy. His name had become a fixture at the top of every leader board, his answers routinely read aloud by professors as the gold standard, and his meticulously organized notes circulated like sacred texts the night before exams. Mathematics was his native tongue; logic, his playground. While others wrestled with abstract theorems and convoluted algorithms, he moved through them with the grace of a poet — as if the numbers whispered their secrets only to him. Complex equations didn't intimidate him; they obeyed him, danced beneath his fingers with the elegance of music under a maestro's baton.

And yet, beyond the neatly ordered world of academics, Raghavendra moved like a stranger in a land that never quite made sense to him. The rhythm of the world — its films, its cricket matches, its trending topics — barely brushed against his consciousness. He wasn't dismissive, nor did he carry the arrogance of superiority; he simply... didn't connect. Ask him the name of a lead actor or the score of the latest match, and he might offer a vague answer, almost apologetically. It wasn't ignorance — it was disinterest, the kind born not out of contempt but of a mind wholly occupied elsewhere.

To Raghavendra, such things seemed fleeting — noise in a world where he sought clarity.

His indifference extended beyond entertainment into the realm of appearances. Fashion was a language he never learned to speak. During Incident, the college's grand cultural fest, when students adorned themselves in their finest — from crisp shirts and statement shoes to perfectly styled hair — Raghavendra strolled in wearing a faded track pant, a shapeless T-shirt, and the kind of well-worn slippers that suggested comfort had long outlived style. His hair stood rebelliously, untouched by comb or care. He moved through the sea of sequins and cologne like a monochrome figure in a Technicolor dream — impossible to miss, yet entirely unmoved.

When someone, half in jest and half in curiosity, asked him why he hadn't made an effort to dress up, he responded with serene conviction:

"Clothes don't add value to me. People already know who I am — and if they don't, a better T-shirt won't help."

There was no conceit in his voice, only truth — a truth many couldn't understand. To him, value resided in intellect, in ideas, in quiet efficiency. Not in branding, not in charm.

Yet for all his detachment from the social world, Raghavendra was far from cold. He possessed a rare, unassuming kindness — the kind that never sought recognition. If a classmate was struggling with code, he'd lean in, offer help, never condescending, never impatient. His brilliance never came with a need to flaunt it. He did not need admiration, applause, or approval. He seemed to live by a different metric — one governed by internal clarity rather than external validation.

In many ways, Pai was like a background process in a complex system — always running, quietly essential, rarely noticed for its quiet strength. There was a certain innocence in his obliviousness, a purity in his focus. He was a man of depth in a world often obsessed with surfaces — a constant in a world of fleeting trends, a mind untouched by the static of distraction.

And though many couldn't quite figure him out, those who took the time to look past the surface discovered something rare: a soul tuned not to the noise of the crowd, but to the quiet brilliance of thought.

Hema found herself spending a great deal of time in the company of Raghavendra Pai — drawn not just to his intellect, but to the quiet confidence that radiated from his composed, brilliant mind. Being around someone so academically gifted gave her a sense of pride, almost as if his wisdom rubbed off on her by proximity. Deep down, she nursed a quiet hope that one day, he would turn to her with more than just notes or logical insights — that he would, perhaps, express the feelings she believed might be hidden beneath his calm attitude.

And yet, a part of her was restless.

Hema often wondered if a life with someone like Pai — for all his brilliance — would allow her the vibrancy she longed for. Though they made a perfect match on paper, she feared that such a relationship might confine her adventurous spirit, her hunger for exploration and spontaneity. There was something missing — a spark, an edge, a sense of being fully alive.

In contrast, there was Ramesh — the campus athlete, a charismatic presence on the field and off. A passionate sportsman and dedicated bodybuilder, he carried himself with an energy that was infectious. Though not exceptional in academics, he navigated his studies with just enough effort to get by, preferring instead to embrace the full spectrum of campus life — from late-night chats under starlit skies to impromptu treks and weekend adventures. With him, life felt electric.

In truth, Hema and Ramesh were a natural match in temperament. Their personalities complemented each other — her intellectual curiosity balanced by his zest for life, her structure softened by his spontaneity. They shared a bond that was easy, alive, and often unspoken. And yet, it remained undefined.

Ramesh, for all his boldness on the sports field, struggled to express the feelings he held for her. Her closeness to Pai — the ever-focused, ever-serious scholar — made Ramesh hesitate. Time and again, he found himself on the verge of confessing his love, only to pull back, convinced she would never see him the way she saw Pai. In his mind, he had already accepted defeat, believing she belonged to a world of ambition and academic brilliance — a world he felt only loosely tethered to.

And so, their story lingered in that uncertain space between possibility and silence — a quiet ache on both sides, waiting to be given a voice.

In stark contrast, there was Suryakanth Patil — the son of a well-known politician, whose presence on campus felt more like a brief detour than a serious academic pursuit. He wasn't there to study or to build a career; he was simply passing time, biding his days until the next election cycle, where he expected to inherit a seat of influence as easily as one inherits a family name.

Surya was flamboyant and unapologetically extravagant. He lived life with excess — luxury cars, designer clothes, and a sense of entitlement that came from never having to earn what he possessed. Charisma cloaked his intentions, but behind the polished exterior was a man driven by self-interest and unchecked desire. When he noticed Hema, it wasn't love that stirred in him, but a shallow infatuation disguised as affection. He pursued her not out of genuine emotion, but because she was beautiful, intelligent, and perhaps unattainable — and that made her a challenge worth chasing. Loyalty was not in his nature. To Surya, women were conquests, not companions. His interest in Hema was fleeting, driven by ego more than emotion. With his wealth and connections, finding attention was never difficult. Girls came easily to him, but Hema's poise and quiet strength made her stand out — and that only fuelled his determination. Yet beneath the charm and easy confidence, it was clear: Hema was just another name on his long list of temporary fascinations.

Hema was undeniably one of the most admired girls on campus — the kind who effortlessly drew attention, not just for her beauty, but for the quiet confidence with which she carried herself. Though she came from a modest, middle-class background, Hema walked with the grace of someone who knew her worth. She was bold, dignified, and fiercely self-assured — the kind of woman who would never compromise her values or dilute her personality to fit someone else's expectations. She could have chosen anyone. There wasn't a single boy who would have said no to her — yet ironically, most never gathered the courage to approach her, convinced that they would be rejected before they even tried. There was a certain myth built around her — that she sought the impossible combination: Pai's intellect, Ramesh's physique, and Surya's wealth.

But what they failed to understand was that Hema didn't measure people by superficial traits alone. She valued substance, loyalty, and depth. And in that regard, both Pai and Ramesh stood apart — sincere, trustworthy, and grounded in their own ways. Surya, with all his charm and money, lacked what mattered most to her: integrity.

To the world, she was the girl who had everything — looks, intelligence, choices. But within, she was someone still searching — not for perfection, but for someone who saw her not as a prize, but as a person.

Years Later…

A few years down the line, during one of the campus recruitment drives, Hema was selected by a leading global software firm. Her brilliance was evident — but so was her grace and presence. She carried herself with such quiet magnetism that it was hard not to notice her, especially for someone like the company's young CEO. Charmed by her intelligence and captivated by her personality, he didn't take long to express his interest. During her probation period itself, he proposed — and she, perhaps swept by the unexpected turn in her life, accepted. They married soon after. On the surface, it looked like the perfect ending — a storybook romance sealed with success, charm, and a promising future.

Meanwhile, the boys who once filled the chapters of her college life — Pai, Ramesh, and Surya — drifted along the natural currents of time.

Pai, true to his quiet brilliance, secured a stable job that matched his intellect. He married a fellow graduate — a kind, grounded woman who chose to dedicate herself to building a home rather than a career. Together, they lived a simple, content life, removed from the chaos of ambition.

Ramesh turned his passion into profession, founding a state-of-the-art fitness centre. His charisma and energy attracted a loyal clientele — and among them, a young woman who would become his partner in both workouts and life. They married, building a bond over shared goals and mutual respect.

Surya, as expected, stepped into politics. Backed by lineage and connections, he carved his way into the public sphere and married a soft-spoken woman from another influential political family — a union shaped more by strategy than love, yet seemingly steady.

Each of them — the dreamers, the rebels, the achievers — had once tasted freedom, friendship, and infatuation in the golden years of college. But as life demanded, they adapted. They grew. They moved on. And they seemed, on the outside, content.

But life has its ironies.

Hema, who once seemed to have found her fairy tale, slowly began to see cracks in the illusion. The man she married — admired by many for his success and status — began to show a different face. Power had changed him. Or perhaps, revealed who he had always been.

With each passing day, his flirtations grew bolder. Every new recruit, every attractive employee, seemed to catch his wandering eye. Shielded by his position, he operated with impunity, his charm now a mask for something far more calculating.

He was no longer just a CEO. He was a man who had learned to manipulate his power, using it to serve his ego, not his ethics. What once seemed like a happy ending had quietly unravelled into something far more complicated — a cautionary tale dressed in success.

A Shift in Silence: Hema's Awakening

At first, Hema tried to look past it — the subtle glances, the casual flirtations, the whispers that floated through office corridors like invisible warnings. She convinced herself it was just corporate noise, the kind that follows men in power. She had always believed in giving the benefit of doubt.

But over time, the pattern became impossible to ignore. The sparkle in his eye for every newcomer, the late-night "strategy meetings" with no minutes recorded, the way his tone changed when speaking to women he wanted to impress. Hema, the same woman who once believed in his charm, began to see it for what it truly was — not charisma, but control; not affection, but appetite.

He was not the man she thought she had married.

And as the truth crystallized, something in her shifted.

This was not the life she had envisioned. She hadn't spent years building herself — her mind, her values, her quiet dignity — only to become a trophy in someone else's power game. The girl who once dreamed of exploring the world, who had refused to compromise her personality for anyone, began to reawaken within her.

She stopped waiting for change. She started creating it.

She focused fiercely on her work — not to gain his attention, but to build her own name, her own credibility. She forged connections outside his shadow, earned respect in rooms where his name didn't carry hers. She remembered what it meant to be her own force — the same woman who had once been admired by Pai for her intellect, matched by Ramesh for her energy, and desired by Surya for her strength.

But this time, she wasn't defined by any of them.

One evening, standing by her apartment window, city lights sprawling before her like a network of choices, Hema made a quiet vow to herself:

"This is not how my story ends — as someone's afterthought, someone's possession. I will rise again. Not in rebellion, but in clarity."

She didn't leave in a storm. She left in strength.

Her exit wasn't dramatic, but it was definitive — a resignation letter, a separation, and then a new beginning. No interviews, no explanations. Just a woman choosing herself.

And somewhere in the quiet, the story took a new shape — not a fairy tale, but something far more powerful: a tale of rediscovery.

Reunion

They all joined for their reunion after 25 years of their graduation. Everyone was happy to prove that they have succeeded in their chosen career and eager to tell their stories. Some were maintaining aloofness, just show that they don't have to prove it with anyone. The weak students in the batch who made it bigger in life were bubbling to share their success stories. On the open dais, pai, Ramesh and Surya expressed that they had crush towards Hema- which naturally male has the gut to express it in front of everyone unlike female counterpart. Boys can tell their past very boldly, but girls cannot take such risk in front of their husbands and kids.

Full Circle

Hema, now a poised and self-assured woman, stood quietly at the edge of the alumni reunion, observing the whirl of music, laughter, and dancing around her. She was no longer the girl waiting to be chosen, nor the young bride chasing a fairy tale. She was Hema — a divorcee, a survivor, a teacher of life, running a well-regarded Personality Development Centre, a space where young minds were shaped with wisdom, confidence, and resilience.

Her coaching centre had a curious but powerful tagline — "Melt into who you are." It reflected the essence of what she had learned and now taught: that personality wasn't something to be worn, like an outfit, but something to be uncovered, like truth beneath layers of fear, failure, and facade. As she stood under the shimmering lights, watching her former classmates sway to old songs, clink glasses, and relive moments of youth, a quiet reflection stirred within her.

"Life," she thought, "is nothing but a cylinder made of many circles. No matter who you are — doctor or dropout, born into wealth or simplicity, from the north, south, east, or west — we all follow the same geometry. Our lives are stacked, one experience upon another, forming a structure shaped not by the radius of our beginnings, but by the height of how far we grow."

Then her mind drifted to something she used to love in her youth — the formula of a cylinder:

$$V=\pi r^2 h$$

It wasn't just math anymore. It was philosophy.

She smiled softly as she extended the thought: "We are like ice," she mused, "no matter how solid or vast, we all eventually melt — and in that melting, we return to water, to our essence. Some melt quickly, surrendering to life's warmth. Some remain frozen, untouched by change. Others melt slowly, part by part, adapting over time. But it's the water we become — the volume of kindness, wisdom, and resilience we release — that truly nurtures the world around us."

At that moment, someone mentioned it was 3:15 a.m. — just one minute past π, the mathematical symbol that had shaped so much of her reflection. She chuckled quietly at the poetry of it.

Then, unexpectedly, a hand gently touched her shoulder from behind. She turned, and there stood Surya, with the same sharp suit, the same arrogant grin — but years older, maybe wiser, maybe not.

"Tell me, Hema," he asked with a smirk, "is my personality good enough now?"

Before she could respond, a commotion broke out nearby — Pai, overwhelmed by nostalgia or perhaps too much drink, had gotten sick in the corner, and Ramesh, ever the practical one, was helping clean up with quiet grace.

But when people looked back, Hema and Surya had vanished into the shadows of the moment — their past unresolved, their present unclear.

The music played on. The night continued to swirl around circles — of memory, of longing, of people still trying to figure out who they were in a world that never stopped spinning.

"Love lessens woman's delicacy and increases man's —Jean Jacques Rousseau"

P(y)arallel Lines

It was exactly 7:30 in the evening. His mind wasn't on dinner or the usual hostel buzz. He was still scrambling to arrange a modest sum—just a hundred rupees. Not for survival, not for something essential, but for something far more irrational yet profoundly important to him at that moment: a greeting card. A card for one of his classmates, Ms. Vandana.

With only a few coins in his pocket and a head full of dreams, he began walking—almost three kilo meters—from his hostel to the nearest Archies Gallery. It wasn't just a walk; it was a quiet pilgrimage of hope, confusion, and longing. There, among rows of glittering cards, he found the one that seemed perfect. Not because it was the most beautiful, but because it carried a message that was bold, teasing, and just the right shade of mischief. The front of the card read, "If you open this New Year card, you will have to give me a big kiss." And inside, "If I knew it was so easy, I would have asked for something bigger."

He bought it for ₹70, clutching it like a secret too precious to share. With only ₹1.50 left, he walked all the way back to the hostel. But the exhaustion of the walk didn't matter—his mind was already spinning with anticipation, self-doubt, and excitement. Could he really give this card to her? Was it too forward? Too risky? Would she laugh, blush, be offended—or worse, tell someone?

He rehearsed scenarios in his mind, each ending differently. As his hostel mates geared up for the usual New Year's Eve celebration, he found himself distant and distracted. While others danced and cheered, he stood apart, dressed and ready—not for the party, but for a moment he had imagined a hundred times. He wasn't celebrating the end of the year. He was waiting for her. Waiting for the courage. Waiting for fate to align in his favour. Because for him, that card wasn't just a playful gesture. It was a silent confession, a trembling hope wrapped in shiny paper and sealed with nervous energy.

The hostel had erupted into chaos and celebration the previous night. Firecrackers, laughter, loud music, and the rhythmic clatter of dancing feet filled the corridors well past midnight. But amidst all that noise, Sanju—worn out by excitement, anxiety, and the emotional weight of his mission—had dozed off unintentionally. The party raged on, but his dreams were filled with unfinished business, with images of a greeting card, a smile he had imagined a thousand times, and the unspoken words he'd hoped to deliver.

Morning crept in unnoticed. The first light had already touched the hostel walls when Sanju woke up with a start. It was 8:30 am. A sense of urgency gripped him—not for class, but for something far more pressing. He immediately looked for the greeting card he had carefully chosen for Vandana. But it was gone.

Panic struck like a bolt. He flung open the drawers, sifted through books, clothes, and every possible nook of the room. Nothing. He turned to his roommate, Vinay, still buried under the blanket, reeking of leftover celebration and groaning from a hangover.

"Vinay! Have you seen my greeting card?" Sanju's voice cracked with anxiety.

Vinay barely opened an eye, mumbled incoherently, and shrugged. "Greeting card? What card?" he slurred.

"There's no concept of locks in these hostels," Sanju thought bitterly. The doors and cupboards were always left open. But this was a close-knit group, built on unspoken trust. Vinay was his confidant—mischievous, yes—but loyal to the bone. He didn't suspect him. Yet the card was missing, and Sanju's heart was racing.

Determined, he went from block to block of the hostels, asking everyone he came across. But no one had seen it. Some were still asleep. Some mocked him lightly, unaware of the storm inside him. To others, it was just a card. To Sanju, it was the bridge between silence and confession.

Crushed and disoriented, Sanju decided not to go to college that day. What was the point, he thought, without the one thing he had built his courage around for days?

By now, Vinay had crawled out of bed, freshened up, and was already getting ready. He slung his backpack lazily over his shoulder and tried to convince Sanju to come along.

"Let's go, man. Come on... let's wish Vandana," he teased, his usual charm on full display.

But Sanju didn't budge. His mood was dark, and he barely responded. Vinay shrugged it off, cracked a joke or two, and walked off, waving like nothing had happened.

He reached the college well past noon, the sun blazing overhead. He roamed around the department first, then made his way to the library. No sign of her. He finally settled himself in the corridor, casually leaning against a pillar. And then, like a slow-motion scene out of a film, Vandana arrived.

She walked in wearing a graceful dress, the kind that made people turn twice. Her smile was as radiant as ever, and she was surrounded by her usual circle of friends, giggling and chatting.

Vinay, ever the flamboyant flirt, walked up confidently.

"Hey Vandana!" he called out with a grin. "Guess what—I have something special for you today!"

Her friends giggled, expecting something light—maybe chocolates or an ice cream treat, as he often offered. "For me?" she said playfully, raising her eyebrows.

"Yes, only for you," Vinay winked, pulling something out of his backpack.

It was the same greeting card.

The very card Sanju had walked miles to buy.

The one with the cheeky message. The one he had saved every rupee for. The one he was too exhausted to protect.

Vinay held it up like it was his own, oblivious—or perhaps not—to the meaning it carried for someone else.

Vandana's eyes sparkled with amusement as she opened it. Her friends burst into laughter at the cheeky lines inside. And Vinay stood there, soaking in the attention.

Back in the hostel, Sanju sat on his bed, staring blankly out the window. A day that was supposed to start with hope had ended in silent heartbreak.

Days turned into weeks, and what began as a harmless prank or perhaps a misguided gesture from Vinay slowly blossomed into something real. Vandana, amused at first, began to notice the persistence in Vinay's playful charm, his unapologetic boldness, and his ever-present laughter that lit up any room. What she once brushed off as casual flirtation began to grow roots. They started spending more time together—library chats, evening walks, sharing chai during free periods. The college began to notice too. Slowly but surely, Vandana and Vinay became Vinay-Vandana—a pair so inseparable that even professors smiled knowingly when they passed by.

Back in the hostel, Sanju remained a silent spectator. He watched the story unfold like an audience member in a play where he was meant to be the protagonist but never walked on stage. He never told anyone the card was his—not even Vinay. He buried it deep, under layers of pride, fear, and heartbreak. At first, it was hard to see them together. But time has its own strange mercy—it doesn't erase pain, but it dulls the edges.

Sanju was never the loudest voice in the room, but he had an eye that saw what others missed—a gaze that lingered just a little longer on fleeting smiles and unspoken emotions. His camera was his companion, a silent keeper of memories and a buffer between him and the world he couldn't fully reach. And through that lens, he found the courage to stay close to the very people who, unknowingly, were carving a hollow in his heart.

He became the unofficial photographer of the group. Whenever there was a picnic, a college fest, a casual get-together in the campus garden—Sanju was always there, camera slung across his shoulder, quietly clicking away. Everyone smiled for his camera, but his focus was unwavering. His frame often settled—almost instinctively—on Vandana.

He would wait for moments when she tilted her head to laugh, or when her eyes crinkled at the corners. He captured those expressions not just as photographs, but as fragments of a dream he dared not pursue. And then, alongside her in the same frame, there was always Vinay—unapologetically cheerful, his arm around her shoulder, his grin wide and effortless.

Sanju spent much of his modest pocket money on buying film rolls. While others used their cash for movies, snacks, or weekend fun, Sanju walked to the old photography studio tucked behind the market street, paid for the development of every roll, and waited patiently for the prints. Not because anyone asked him to. Not because he was going to be paid. But because when he handed over those photos to Vandana and saw her eyes light up, when he saw her smile as she nudged Vinay and laughed at their silly poses, something inside him felt oddly complete—and equally broken.

He was the invisible artist behind their visible love.

He told himself that her happiness was enough. That the joy he saw on her face was a gift, even if it came at the cost of his own. But in truth, with every click of the shutter, he was capturing not just their memories—but the slow unravelling of his own hope. The camera didn't lie, and neither did the silence in his heart.

Vinay would sometimes ruffle his hair, thanking him for the pictures. Vandana would say, "Sanju, you have magic in your fingers." And Sanju would smile. Because what else could he do?

Love had passed him by, right in front of his eyes. And yet, he chose to keep clicking—because sometimes, helplessness doesn't come from not being able to act. It comes from loving so deeply that you give, even when it empties you.

One rainy afternoon, long after their college days, someone casually asked Sanju during a reunion, "Hey… do you ever wonder what would've happened if you had given that card to Vandana?"

Sanju smiled faintly, looking away for a second, then said:

"If I had proposed her, maybe she would've smiled politely, accepted the card, and forgotten it the next day. Or maybe she would've laughed and told her friends—it might've embarrassed her. Or… perhaps… just perhaps, she would've given me the chance to show how deeply I cared."

But love… love isn't just about who reaches first. It's about who fits.

Vinay was loud, impulsive, fearless. I was quiet, hesitant, thoughtful. Maybe I was meant to love her silently. Maybe she was meant to be with someone who could say everything I only rehearsed. In one of the classes, the teacher wrote a line on the board and challenged the students, "How can you make this line shorter?" Before anyone could even blink, Vinay confidently responded, "By drawing a longer line above or below it."

The class chuckled, impressed by his wit.

What no one knew was that these clever little gems often came from Sanju. But Vinay, ever sharp and opportunistic, had the knack for knowing exactly when to use them—making himself look effortlessly smart in the moment.

I don't regret falling for her. I only regret not trying. Because sometimes, even if love doesn't succeed, courage should."

There was a pause.

And then he added, with a smirk, "But if I had given her that card… Vinay wouldn't be the one holding her hand now." Sanju places the headphones over his ears, letting the song wash over his silence and the Ellie Goulding's song goes on…

"Yeah, I'll let you set the pace,
Cause I'm not thinking straight'
My head's spinning around, I can't see clear no more, What are you waiting for?
Love me like you do…la la… love me like you do."

Be **Strong**—but, not rude.
Be **Kind**—but, not weak.
Be **Humble**—but, not shy.
Be **Proud**—but, not arrogant.

Bermuda Triangle

The gleaming car pulled up gracefully in front of the college auditorium, catching the attention of everyone gathered for the much-awaited cultural fest. As the door opened, time seemed to slow. Draped in a flowing silk saree that shimmered with every step, a woman descended with an air of timeless elegance. Her every move carried the grace of a dancer, her presence a blend of poise and power. She was none other than 'Shakuntala Kuduva'—a renowned classical dancer and an admired cultural icon of the region. She had been invited as the guest of honour and chief judge for the intercollegiate dance competition.

The air buzzed with whispers, admiration, and awe. Heads turned, and hearts paused for a moment.

In the same auditorium, a familiar figure moved through the crowd—Dr. Anand, a beloved lecturer in the college. His warmth, wit, and vibrant spirit had made him a favourite among students and colleagues alike. He was a singer, a performer, an effortless host who made any college event come alive. And yes—he was a married man.

But today, something inside him wavered. For months now, he had admired Shakuntala from a quiet distance. Not just for her art, but for the mystery in her eyes, the calm in her voice, the confidence with which she carried herself. She belonged to an illustrious family and was married to a reputed businessman—but to Anand, she was more than her identity. She was the kind of woman whose presence lingered even after she had walked past.

Every time she spoke to him with grace and warmth, his heart fluttered—not with lust, but with the tender ache of a man who feared that admiration could one day cross the line into longing. He respected her immensely, but also feared himself. *What if, someday, words slipped that he couldn't take back?*

That day, Anand arrived at the fest with his wife by his side—a graceful woman in her own right, calm and content. As they stepped in, one of Anand's most outspoken students, Bob Kennedy, came bounding up to greet them. Known for his curious mind and sharp tongue, Bob leaned closer to Anand's wife with a teasing glint in his eye.

Pointing toward the dazzling Shakuntala, he said with a boyish smirk, "Madam, that dancer seems to really like

Anand Sir…"

He waited, expecting a flicker of jealousy. Maybe even a gasp.

But what he got instead was a smile—soft, confident, and filled with something far deeper than mere amusement.

She turned to Bob and said, "I'm happy. It means my husband is admired by beautiful and graceful women. What more could I wish for? He is mine."

Her words didn't carry sarcasm or possessiveness. They were spoken with quiet pride and profound love—the kind that didn't need to mark territory because it knew its strength. Anand glanced at her, stunned. It was the kind of moment that rearranged a man's heart. He felt seen, understood, and grounded.

Bob, momentarily speechless, realized he had just witnessed something rare: not drama, but dignity. No doubt, but devotion.

As the echoes of his wife's words settled around him, something shifted in Anand—not in thunder or lightning, but like the silent turn of a key inside a locked room.

"I'm happy. It means my husband is admired by beautiful and graceful women. What more could I wish for? He is mine."

Her words weren't wrapped in jealousy. There was no bitterness, no sarcasm hiding between syllables. It was simply said—with a smile full of faith, and eyes that didn't flinch. That unwavering calm hit Anand harder than any confrontation could have.

She knew.

She had always known.

Not the details. Not the quiet stirrings he tried to suppress when Shakuntala walked into a room. But she had sensed the drift. The soft sway of his attention. The pause in his voice when he spoke of the dancer. The unspoken energy.

And yet… she chose trust.

She didn't accuse, didn't control, didn't crumble. She stood tall, like the shoreline—watching the waves flirt with the wind, but knowing the ocean would always return to her.

It was in that moment Anand felt small and significant all at once. Small in the face of her grace. Significant because *he mattered* to someone so rare.

He had admired Shakuntala's beauty, her artistry, her aura. Yes, she was magnetic. And yes, he had been drawn.

But now, as he looked at his wife—simple, sincere, and proud—he saw something else:

The kind of love that doesn't beg for attention, because it has already given you everything.

It wasn't guilt that rose in Anand's chest. It was awakening. A deeper kind of love, not loud or poetic, but rooted. He realized then that loyalty wasn't just a promise made at a wedding altar. It was a daily choice—a discipline of the heart.

He turned to her that evening with fresh eyes. The lines on her face weren't from time, they were from shared laughter. Her worn-out bangles were not lack of luxury, but quiet sacrifices made in the name of "us." Her plainness, once overlooked, now felt like poetry.

And within him, a quiet vow formed—not shouted, not scribbled in a diary, not sealed with ceremony. Just a silent, sacred resolve:

"No more wandering glances.
No more temptations dressed as admiration.
From this moment on,
my heart learns to stay where it truly belongs."

As the cultural fest wound down and guests began to take their leave, a quiet stillness returned to the auditorium—like the hush that follows a great storm. Dr.

Anand was standing near the backstage corridor, caught in a rare moment of inward stillness, when Sharan Biradar, one of his enthusiastic students, approached him.

"Sir," he asked, "should we escort Madam Shakuntala back to her home, like we did last time?"

Anand looked at Sharan for a moment. It was an innocent question, born from routine. A simple courtesy.

But inside Anand, the moment was anything but simple.

Just weeks ago, he would've taken the opportunity himself. To walk beside her, even briefly, felt like moving within a dream—close enough to feel the warmth of a flame, yet always pretending it didn't burn. He had done it before—accompanied her, conversed with her, floating in that vague space between admiration and temptation.

And yet… today felt different.

He smiled, but it wasn't his usual charming smile. It was softer. Quieter. Almost like an apology to himself.

"No, Sharan," he said gently. "That won't be necessary."

Sharan nodded and left, unaware that those two letters—No—were Anand's first real act of loyalty, not to his wife, but to himself.

Anand and his wife returned home late in the evening. The long day of the college fest, the conversations, the applause, and the quiet wars within had drained them both. They barely spoke. A shared silence followed them into the bedroom, not awkward—but familiar, like an old blanket that no longer needed straightening.

She fell asleep within minutes, curled on her side, her hand still resting near his shoulder. But Anand remained wide awake. Eyes open. Breathing slow. Thoughts racing.

Outside the window, the wind picked up. And in his ears, louder than the ceiling fan, louder than the passing autos—was the sound of the Arabian Sea.

Except… they weren't near the coast. The sea wasn't audible from their neighbourhood. And yet, in his mind, it was roaring. Calling.

He closed his eyes and suddenly found himself standing on the sands of Panambur Beach, barefoot, the moonlight painting silver shadows on the waves. The sky was heavy, the sea restless. He stood there, watching, but never stepping forward.

He was afraid.

Not of water—but of what water could hide.

He remembered once reading about the Bermuda Triangle—that cursed stretch of sea where compasses spin without direction, where maps become meaningless, and even the most seasoned captains vanish without a trace. A place where logic drowns, and no one truly returns the same.

Standing now at the edge of his own emotional storm, Anand felt like he had wandered dangerously close to that mythical vortex—not in the ocean, but in his soul.

He hadn't been pulled in.
He hadn't sunk.

But the fear still gripped him.

Because for a moment, he had felt its pull—seductive, powerful, and terrifying. And yet somehow… by sheer will or by a whisper of grace, he had turned away.

Now, lying awake in the quiet of dawn, the roar of invisible waves still echoing in his mind, Anand didn't feel victorious.

He felt like a man washed ashore—drenched, breathless, and shaken—a lone survivor from a shipwreck no one knew had happened.

And he knew one thing for sure:

Next time, he might not make it back.

"That's what temptation is," he thought. "A tide that looks calm until it pulls you under."

He stayed on the shore, resisting the need to wade in. But his heart… it felt wet. Heavy. Stirred.

The next day, sunlight pierced through the curtains like an unexpected guest. Anand stirred, exhausted from a sleepless night.

From the washing area, his wife's voice rang out, playful yet annoyed.

"How many times do I have to tell you, Anand? "Not to wear the jeans to the beach!"

Look at all the sand you've brought into the washing machine!" He smiled faintly. The kind of smile that hides more than it reveals.

But then… he froze.

His eyes darted to the corner of the room, where his jeans lay folded over the chair. He hadn't touched them since last week.

"He hadn't worn them to the beach."

Because he never went to the beach. He had only dreamed of it… hadn't he?

He slowly got up, walked to the jeans. Reached into the pocket. His fingers touched something. Gritty. Damp. Sand. Cold, sea-scented, and very real.

"Where is your Bermuda *Chaddi*-the half pant' his wife asked. He smiled and asked her "What did you say…did you say 'Bermuda Triangle?'

She shouts "No..Bermuda *Chaddi*."

Anand stood in front of the map hanging in the study room, his eyes slowly drifting toward the mysterious patch of ocean labelled 'Bermuda Triangle,' as if searching for answers hidden in its depths.

“Practice makes man perfect. Make sure that you chose the right method—Magada”

On the DOT.

Manoj, known to friends as Manu, is the kind of guy who makes an impression the moment he walks into a room—tall, charming, with effortless good looks, and a disarming smile. His hostel room wall is a collage of world-famous models and dream destinations—more like a manifestation board than decoration. To him, life is meant to be grand, and love should be something out of a movie.

But here's the twist—he rarely acts on time. His ambitions are skyscraper-high, but his discipline is somewhere on ground level. Assignments are submitted late, meetings missed, and even his best friends have stopped checking their watches when he says, “I'll be there in 5.” In some instances, his friends stopped taking him seriously. If he comes ok; if he doesn't turn up is also ok.

Despite that, there's something deeply sincere about him. His laziness isn't born from arrogance—it's the by-product of being lost in his own mind, constantly dreaming, constantly distracted by "what could be." Yet, amidst all his fantasies and posters of exotic beauty queens, it's Meera—the "ordinary-looking good girl"—who anchors his heart.

He's terrified. Not of the world or the unknown—but of losing Meera while chasing everything else.

On the contrary, Meera is studious, time conscious and punctual. The Realist with a Clock in Her Heart Meera isn't someone who turns heads at first glance. But when she speaks, people listen—not because she demands it, but because she's cantered, composed, and confident in her quiet ways. She's the kind of girl who highlights her notes in different colours, shows up five minutes early, and sets goals in bullet points.

Her world isn't small—it's focused. While others roam looking for meaning, she finds joy in small victories: finishing a novel, helping a friend, or watching the sunrise with a cup of coffee. She doesn't need the world to admire her. Her own reflection in the mirror and the rhythm of her ticking watch are enough.

And yet, she's drawn to Manu—the boy who forgets time, forgets things, but never forgets to make her smile.

Deep down, she wonders:
Will I always have to wait for him? Or will he ever learn to show up—on the dot—for the one thing that truly matters?

The sprawling campus of the Coastal School of Architecture in Mangalore had seen its share of love stories—most fleeting, some forgettable. But no one quite noticed the silent tug-of-war between Manoj and Meera.

They were both in their final year of B.Arch., but they might as well have come from two different planets. Manu, as everyone called him, had the look of someone destined for greatness—tall, handsome, slightly dishevelled in a way that made it look deliberate. There were photographs of international models pinned above his study table, not as inspiration but as silent trophies he imagined winning someday.

But if charm was his birth right, punctuality was his nemesis.

Manu lived in delays. Alarm clocks meant nothing to him. Timelines were elastic. Professors groaned at his brilliance wasted on late submissions, and friends laughed when he promised to be "there in five." He rarely was.

And yet, Meera—the topper, the time-keeper, the one who colour-coded her folders and ticked off tasks like a machine—liked him.

No one understood why. Maybe she didn't either.

She had a quiet elegance, a strong spine, and eyes that didn't flinch when challenged. Where Manu drifted in dreams, Meera stood anchored in her reality. But when she looked at him—really looked—it was with a gaze that held a peculiar blend of admiration and disappointment.

"If he could just be on time," she once muttered to herself, "he'd be unstoppable."

Their final semester brought the much-anticipated dissertation project. A ticket to the professional world. Everyone wanted a unique site to study. Manu had his heart set on 'The Arena', a sports complex in Manipal, renowned for its futuristic design.

He had even secured an appointment with the Dean to request site access. Meera was impressed—for a moment.

Until he showed up thirty minutes late.

"They were never going to allow me anyway," he muttered, kicking a pebble as they walked back from class. "They're always polite to girls. That's how it works."

Meera stopped. She turned to face him squarely.

"They're polite to people who respect time, Manu. You didn't."

Her tone was calm, but it cut deeper than any shout could have. He said nothing, just looked at her—the way he always did when he knew she was right and hated her for it.

But this was their rhythm.

They argued. They worked late nights on designs. They shared filter coffee from the canteen that always had too much sugar. Sometimes, they sat under the old banyan tree behind the studio block, where ideas flowed more freely than words.

"Why do you care so much if I'm late?" he asked once, half-serious.

Meera didn't look up from her sketchbook.

"Because I hate to see someone waste potential. Especially yours."

He didn't respond. Just smiled faintly and watched her sketch, wondering why the most disciplined person he knew still had time for someone like him.

Their story hadn't begun. Not really.

But maybe—just maybe—it was waiting for that one moment.

That one time he'd show up 'on the dot.'

They completed their project. They earned their degrees. What they didn't anticipate was how love—true, deep, unsettling love—would become their biggest challenge.

Falling for each other wasn't the problem. They had crossed that bridge long ago, somewhere between midnight design sessions and coffee-fuelled studio arguments. It was the world outside their college gates that threw stones in their path.

Meera, with her head held high and a fierce fire in her eyes, was ready to face her family. She had never shied away from bold choices. Convincing her parents about Manu? She believed she could do it. After all, love wasn't a crime.

But Manu's side of the story was different. His father was a rigid, short-tempered man who wore his pride like a badge. The idea of his son marrying a North Indian girl from a different caste wasn't just unacceptable—it was unforgivable. His mother, caught between duty and affection, could only cry, whispering about the marriages of Manu's sisters being jeopardized.

And then, a twist Meera didn't expect—her father.

The man she always believed to be liberal, open-minded, and progressive, had already started looking for alliances back in Rajasthan. He didn't consult her. He didn't ask what she wanted. One day, he simply sent her a photo of a prospective groom.

A man who looked more like a round figure than a well-rounded one, wrapped in silk and money.

To Meera, that photo was more than just a suitor—it was a warning: her life decisions were being made without her consent. And the clock was ticking.

Strangely, it wasn't Manu's parents who became the biggest hurdle. It was hers.

Anxiety began to bloom inside her like a wildfire. She couldn't afford to lose control over her life. Not now. Not when she was on the brink of her dreams. She had just received an offer from one of the biggest real estate firms in Dubai. And she knew—waiting even one more week could cost her everything.

Manu, meanwhile, was tangled in hesitation. He loved Meera with all his heart. But he wasn't the kind of man who made radical choices. Chaos scared him. Defying family scared him. Making a move without a "plan" scared him even more.

That's when Meera, bold as ever, made a decision.

"We'll get married. Tomorrow. At Sri Krishna Temple. Then, we'll leave straight for Dubai. If you want me, be there. If you're not… I'll go alone."

Manu blinked, stunned. He had no words, just a knot tightening in his chest.

But he agreed. Not out of courage—but out of confusion, love, fear. A mixture of emotions he couldn't quite name.

Meera, always the planner, laid it all out like a military operation:

Catch the 9:30 am bus at Corporation Circle.

Reach Udupi by 10:30 am.

Take a 10-minute walk to the Sri Krishna Temple.

The wedding rituals would take roughly 90 minutes.

Post-ceremony, hire a taxi to Mangalore International Airport.

Board the 4:00 pm flight to Dubai—as husband and wife.

"Mangalore buses," she reminded him, "run like clockwork. Singapore or Japan couldn't do better."

Now, the only question remained:

Would he make it? Would he be… on the dot?

Naturally, they have enough time—arriving 10 or 20 minutes early or late wouldn't really change much. But when someone is about to do something wrong or socially unacceptable, a strange transformation happens. They become hyper-alert, unusually punctual, almost obsessive about timing. Just like thieves—who, despite their reckless intent, are often the most precise in their actions.
Manu glanced at the clock. 9:12 AM. Still 18 minutes left. He never arrived on time for anything—not classes, not dates, not even exams. But today… he was early. Too early.

Strange, he thought. Why now?

Manu stood at the Corporation Circle, staring at two buses parked ahead of him. The first was half full and about to leave, a driver lazily pulling the gear with one hand and sipping tea with the other. For 17 minutes, he was just imagining his future life at Dubai. It was 9:29 AM. He decided to board the bus which was ready to leave at 9.30 am.

The second was the 9:30 sharp bus to Udupi. That was the one she had told him to take. On the dot, she had said. And for the first time in his life, Manu was exactly on time.

He boarded and slipped into the last seat. The bus, as if aware of its own rhythm, roared to life like a beast uncaged. It surged forward, horns blaring, a declaration of its dominance over Mangalore's chaotic roads. It weaved through autos, motorbikes, fruit carts, and pedestrians as if racing a destiny it couldn't see.

The woman beside him clutched her saree tighter with each bend. Manu didn't notice. His eyes were fixed outside, but his mind was drifting—in ten minutes he would be holding Meera's hand in a temple filled with prayers and quiet rebellion. They would become husband and wife, just like that. It felt surreal. Like a movie. Like a moment borrowed from someone else's life.

At Mulki—*another town 20 km away from the Mangalore city*, someone vacated the front seat, and Manu, not wanting to miss the moment he'd see her from the bus window, moved up. He sat right behind the driver, watching the road stretch endlessly ahead, like fate unrolling a carpet just for them.

Up ahead, a Kerala-registered Benz swerved into view—youngsters, loud, competitive. One of them rolled the window down and hurled a taunt at the driver. The driver, already infamous for his ego, smirked. His grip tightened. The race began—not of speed, but of pride. Mangalore drivers, like their Kerala counterparts, weren't just steering wheels—they were holding on to kingdoms.

And then it happened.

At Katapadi—a small roadside village with Udupi just 9 km away, the bus tried to overtake the car. The road narrowed, the divider loomed—and like many moments in life where ego meets impulse—it cracked.

The bus struck the divider, wheels lifting, screams rising, time stopping. It ricocheted to the left, skidded, and slammed head-on into a massive rain tree.

Three never got up again.

Two were pulled from the mangled car, unrecognizable, young. One—was flung from the bus, the glass giving way like it knew it had to let him go. Manu's body lay twisted in a blur of metal, flesh, and silence. The golden thread on his wrist Meera had tied just a week ago had snapped, dancing in the wind like a farewell. The buses that departed just before and after the 9:30 AM one reached Udupi safely. His phone was ringing. The Katapadi police officer hesitated before answering. A voice, soft and anxious, asked, "Has he reached?" The officer didn't say much—just silence and explained it one sentence that explained everything. The call disconnected. There are silences in life that speak louder than any cry. For Meera, it was not just the phone call that ended abruptly—it was a chapter, a dream, a life she had imagined down to the dot.

Returning home felt like surrendering to a world that had betrayed her, a place where the walls carried the echoes of wedding bells that never rang. So, she stayed back in Manipal—alone, but not broken. She joined MIT as a lecturer, finding solace in structure, routine, and the sterile certainty of architectural plans. Teaching others how to draw dreams, even as hers lay in ruins.

On a quiet Monday morning, she walked into her 9:30 AM class for third-year B.Arch. students. The world had moved on, indifferent to one love story that had halted at a traffic divider in Katapadi.

Two students—one boy, one girl—entered five minutes late. Normally, she would have raised her voice, made them feel the weight of tardiness. But that day, she simply looked at them… and let it pass.

Because grief changes the way we measure time.

Because when someone you love dies "on the dot," clocks lose their meaning.

At the end of the class, she turned to a student in the front row and casually asked, “What time is it?”

“I think 10:30, ma’am.”

Just then, the electric bell rang.

"Everything will be happy at the end. If it is not happy, it is not an end — Unknown"

Circle

Science itself doesn't change every day—our understanding of it does. What we perceive as breakthroughs are often revelations of truths that have always existed in nature. Through research, we are not creating facts; we are uncovering them. Perhaps that's why it's called 're-search'—a deliberate act of searching again, to find and prove what has long been there, waiting to be seen, tested, and understood through evidence and experimentation.

In much the same way, we must rediscover the love that has always quietly existed among us. As the renowned Kannada poet Dr. G. S. Shivarudrappa beautifully writes, *'Ello huḍukide illada dēvara kallu maṇṇugaḷa guḍiyoḷage, ille iruva prīti prēmagaḷa guruthisadadenu nammoḷage'* — which almost translates to: *'I searched for God in temples of stone and mud, yet failed to recognize the love that already dwells within us.'* His words remind us that what we often seek far and wide may already reside within and around us—only waiting to be truly seen and felt.

Countless times, my mother never had food, just to make sure that we are eaten sufficiently. We have never said thanks. My driver never said he has some problem and he cannot come. He always assured me that everything is fine at his home. The watchman, who earns only a modest salary, never fails to greet me with a warm smile every single day. There's a quiet joy in his eyes—a sense of peace and contentment that's hard to miss. It's not just him. Many others around us—the support staff, the janitors, those who toil behind the scenes for what society calls "Insignificant Wages"—seem to live happier, more content lives than many with far greater means.

How is that possible? What is their secret? It makes me wonder if happiness truly lies in wealth, or if it resides in simpler things—gratitude, purpose, and peace of mind.

My assistant Mrs Sowmya never said that she was burdened with over work. My wife never said that I am boring. Of course at times she might have mentioned; but not on a serious note. Why is she managing me and my weaknesses. One chilly winter morning, around 5:30 AM, I was greeted at the bus stop by one of my juniors, Dr. Manjappa. Despite the biting cold and the early hour, there he was, patiently waiting to receive me. Today, in a more convenient world, I could've easily arranged for a taxi, Ola, or Uber. But back then, such gestures carried a different kind of warmth—something that no app can offer. What joy did he find in doing that? What silent satisfaction did he draw from standing in the dark, cold dawn just to welcome me?

This memory took me even further back—nearly two decades ago—when Dr. Swamy, a fellow student during our Master's program, would unfailingly carry all my notes to class every single day. No one asked him to. No one expected it. Yet he did it, with a kind of quiet loyalty that words often fail to capture.

Then there was Rajanna—my classmate who rarely showed emotions, who seemed almost stoic by nature. But even he had his own way of expressing care. Every morning, before I even woke up, he would press my clothes and keep them ready. He never said a word about it. No grand gestures. Just simple, thoughtful acts that revealed more than any spoken affection ever could.

These memories make me wonder—not just about the acts themselves, but about the invisible bonds, the unspoken respect, and the silent happiness that people find in doing things for others. It's a kind of love that isn't loud, but lingers for a lifetime.

The moment the word *"love"* is uttered, most minds instinctively drift to the image of a boy and a girl—of romance, passion, and companionship. It has become almost automatic, as if the idea of love has been boxed into a narrow, cinematic frame that society projects endlessly. But perhaps *love* is the most misunderstood concept in human consciousness.

Love, in its truest form, is not confined to the corridors of romance. It is not just a relationship status or an emotional exchange between two individuals. It is far more expansive, far more essential. In reality, *love* is a neutral, foundational force—as vital to existence as air or water. It is the first emotion a new-born feels in a mother's touch, the invisible thread that binds a soldier to his homeland, the silent respect between a teacher and a student, the instinctive protection a bird offers its fledgling.

Love is not exclusive—it is inclusive. It is not dependent on physical proximity or passionate intensity—it flows even in absence, and sometimes in silence. It can be in a gesture, in sacrifice, in understanding, or even in letting go. To reduce it to just romance is like seeing only the tip of an iceberg while missing the vast, magnificent mountain beneath the surface.

Philosophically, love is the most neutral and universal language of existence. It is neither masculine nor feminine, neither rich nor poor—it transcends class, caste, culture, and creed. It exists in the roots of a tree stretching deep into the earth, in the devotion of a dog sitting by a grave, and in the quiet company of a friend who says nothing but stays.

Love, when seen this way, is not just an emotion. It is the fundamental element of life itself—the invisible energy that sustains meaning, movement, and memory.

So perhaps it's time we reclaim the word *love* from the narrow definitions we've given it. Let it breathe, let it flow, and let it be seen for what it truly is—a sacred, silent presence that gives life its soul.

Jack—a regal Mudhol Hound, an indigenous breed native to Karnataka—was never just a pet. He was a presence, a companion, a silent yet expressive member of our family. He didn't need to be trained to belong; he just *was*—part of our daily rhythm, part of our emotional fabric.

Every evening, like clockwork, as the sun dipped and I returned home around 6:15 PM, Jack would anticipate my arrival. The moment he sensed my footsteps, he'd dart ahead and claim the bean bag I always used to sit on, almost as if to say, *"Welcome home, I've been waiting."* It wasn't mischief—it was his way of sharing space, of being near.

What struck us most was his sensitivity. Jack could sense our moods—our joys, our anxieties, our silences. He responded not like a trained animal but like a sentient being. He would often stand on his hind legs and embrace my wife, almost human-like in his posture. He was tall, proud, and gentle—and in his own way, affectionate. When we spoke, he'd lock his eyes on us and listen with a kind of undivided attention that many humans fail to offer. He wasn't just hearing; he was *understanding.*

But then came the inevitable bend in the road. We had to move from our Government Quarters to an apartment complex where pets were not allowed. A cruel rule that reduced love to a line in the lease agreement. Jack was temporarily kept at the officers' club, and later, arrangements were made to send him to a coffee estate where someone had agreed to take care of him.

Three days later, when we went to see him one last time, we were told he hadn't eaten a single morsel since we left. That broke something inside us. His eyes—deep, dark, and soulful—spoke a language words never could. There was no barking, no jumping—just a quiet, aching gaze. He was grieving. And so were we.

When it was finally time to hand him over, both my wife and I couldn't hold back our tears. We cried—not just for Jack, but for the unspoken bond, for the love we had to part with against our will. That moment reminded me of my childhood, when my parents used to sell the cows we had raised with care. The farewell always carried the same kind of ache—when love meets helplessness, it wounds deep.

Some connections in life are beyond language, beyond logic. Jack was one of them. He didn't just walk on four legs—he walked right into our hearts, and left pawprints we carry to this day. Even now, the Jack's photo is there in my home at a prominent place.

The core philosophy I wish to reaffirm here is deeply rooted in the principle of *Karma*—the timeless idea that life, in its essence, is a mirror, reflecting back what we put into it. *You get what you give.* This is not just a spiritual cliché or a poetic ideal; it's a rhythm that governs the human experience, often quietly, but unmistakably.

Now, I say this as someone who identifies as an atheist, a scientist—someone who doesn't subscribe to rituals, blind beliefs, or untested dogmas. I don't believe in the supernatural as it's conventionally understood. And yet, even from a scientific perspective, we often find that while 95 to 98 percent of phenomena can be explained, there remains a mysterious margin—those lingering 2 to 5 percent—where logic meets silence, where data yields to the unknown.

It is in that narrow but profound space that I find room to acknowledge a greater force—not necessarily divine in form, but certainly undeniable in function. Whether we name it energy, vibration, resonance, or consciousness, something persists beyond equations. And within that mystery, *Karma* makes sense—not as superstition, but as a natural law of cause and effect, extended beyond the physical.

It's a circle, simple yet profound. What you put out—be it kindness or cruelty, honesty or deceit—will, in time and form, return. It may not follow a timeline that satisfies human impatience, but it is inescapable. Call it a virtuous circle or a vicious one; the truth is, it turns with or without our consent.

And perhaps this is the humbling truth: that in a universe of randomness and reason, there is still a quiet symmetry to life. An unseen ledger that balances itself over time. This belief, if you can call it that, isn't based on faith, but on observation—on lived experiences, on patterns repeated across decades, people, and places.

So while I may not bow to gods, I bow to this principle. Because time and again, life has proved beyond doubt—*you truly get what you give.*

The concept I'm referring to is not as mechanically direct as Newton's Third Law of Motion, which states, *"For every action, there is an equal and opposite reaction."* Life doesn't always respond with immediate symmetry or in predictable ways. It doesn't deal in linear equations. Instead, it moves in *circles.*

In this circular rhythm, what you give doesn't always come back from the same person, in the same way, or at the same time—but it *does* return. Energy, intentions, actions—they revolve around you, quietly weaving the life you experience. You may throw kindness into the world and receive support from an unexpected corner years later. You may sow bitterness and face resistance when you least expect it. The circle turns, slowly but surely.

That's why it becomes essential to be *conscious* of what kind of circle you are creating. The life you live is often the echo of the life you've built, moment by moment, gesture by gesture. If you want peace, give peace. If you seek respect, offer it. If you yearn for love, cultivate it within and around you. The circle you spin today may well be the world you inhabit tomorrow.

So, while life may not obey Newton's laws in the realm of human emotions and experience, it follows its own cosmic pattern—subtle, complex, and circular. And in that circle, you are both the centre, circumference and the creator.

Yours faithfully
—The Circle

"Happiness is key to the success. Not the otherwise. So, be happy —Unknown"

The Square: Metaphor for Life

A square, with its four equal sides and four corners, represents structure, stability, balance, and boundaries—all of which are fundamental to how we live and grow.

Four Corners = Four Phases of Life

Each corner of a square can be seen as a phase or milestone in life:

- **Childhood** – Innocence, learning, dependence.
- **Youth** – Dreams, exploration, rebellion.
- **Adulthood** – Responsibility, achievement, struggle.
- **Old Age** – Reflection, wisdom, detachment.

Life moves from one corner to another. You turn, you shift direction, but eventually, you complete the cycle and come full circle—back to the starting point, but with deeper understanding.

The Edges = Life's Boundaries

The sides of the square represent the boundaries we live within—our values, culture, family, and conscience. Just as a square holds its shape through balance, our lives gain stability when we respect the limits of our choices, relationships, and responsibilities.

If you stretch one side too far (e.g., ambition without ethics, freedom without discipline), the square collapses. A good life, like a perfect square, is about keeping all sides in harmony.

The Centre = The Self

The perfect balance of a square is at its centre. That's where *you* are—your soul, your consciousness. No matter which edge or corner you're close to at any point—career, family, health, or relationships—your sense of *self* must remain cantered for life to feel whole.

Turning Corners = Life's Turning Points

Each time you reach a corner in a square, you must *turn*. These are the moments of change in life—decisions, losses, new beginnings. You can't keep going in the same direction forever; growth comes from learning to turn with grace and move to the next edge.

Square vs. Circle

Unlike a circle, which is endless and smooth, a square has defined direction and abrupt turns. Life is not always fluid—it forces you to pause, pivot, and change course. And yet, like a circle, a square also comes back to the start—just more rigid, more real.

Whether it's a circle or a square, the total degrees remain constant—360. The shape may change, the path may differ, but the essence—the totality of experience—stays the same. Life, in a way, mirrors this geometry. It gives you chances—three, maybe more—before it leads you to that final corner, a place where you're forced to confront yourself.

You may try to outwit it, to pivot at the last moment, to flee from the reckoning. But more often than not, you find yourself trapped in a familiar loop, repeating the same mistakes, haunted by the same choices you tried to outrun. It's almost as if life is *designed* this way—deliberate, measured, inevitable.

The message is subtle but profound: no matter how much you twist and turn, the *sum total of your actions, thoughts, and consequences*—like those 360 degrees—remains complete. The *form* may change, but the *truth* remains. Whether you wander in circles or march squarely toward your goals, life will always bring you full circle, back to where your intentions began.

Meaning, ultimately, you are the constant. The world around you may shift, but the essence of your journey—the karmic balance, the lessons you must learn, the inner reckoning—remains. Life doesn't necessarily punish or reward—it reflects. And until you evolve beyond those repeated patterns, the corners will keep appearing. The circle will keep spinning. And the total sum—of your choices, your growth, your becoming—will always be yours to reckon with.

At the core of human nature lies a complex yearning—a desire to be loved, accepted, and validated. Man, by his inherent disposition, often seeks to extend his emotional investments far and wide. He yearns to be loved by many, to win hearts, to feel wanted. This pursuit brings him a deep sense of satisfaction—almost like a conquest, not always of people, but of affection itself.

Women, on the other hand, tend to be more discerning in matters of the heart. They may not give away their love as casually. Yet, even they—despite emotional intelligence and instinctive caution—sometimes miscalculate, choosing unwisely or trusting the wrong person. No one is immune to the unpredictable tides of love.

What's interesting, however, is how differently men and women often respond when love fails. When things fall apart, it is frequently observed that women find ways to move on—perhaps because nature has endowed them with resilience, or perhaps because society has long taught them to adapt and survive emotionally. Sometimes they genuinely forget; at other times, they master the art of appearing as though they have. They gather themselves and step into new chapters of life, often without looking back.

Men, however, tend to carry the emotional weight longer. A heartbreak can linger in their memory, unresolved, etched deep like a scar. While women may process, heal, and move forward, many men struggle to express, let alone process, their emotional wounds. This contrast is not about strength or weakness—it's about the different ways love takes root in us.

Nature, in its curious wisdom, has given women the evolutionary power of choice. In many ways, they are the selectors, the gatekeepers of emotional and reproductive partnerships. This innate power can make them more intuitive, more strategic—and yes, sometimes more capable of emotional manoeuvring than men. In today's world, if a woman chooses to, she may find multiple suitors in a short span—not merely because of appearance or charm, but because of this ancient biological privilege to choose.

Ultimately, love remains one of the most powerful, unpredictable forces in human life. Both men and women are its seekers and sufferers, its poets and its prisoners. Yet the way they engage with it, and recover from it, often reflects not only their individual personalities but also the deeper patterns etched into our collective human nature.

While it's true that women, due to certain societal dynamics and biological privileges, may possess a greater *potential* to be selective or strategic in matters of love and relationships, it's important to distinguish between potential and intent. Society, often consciously or unconsciously, grants women certain emotional privileges—such as being the pursued rather than the pursuer—which can sometimes offer more flexibility or leverage in romantic situations. This may occasionally create space where manipulation can occur under the guise of love—but that is not a gendered flaw; it is a human one.

However, when it comes to *attempts* at deception or betrayal in love, it is often men who initiate more frequently. This could be rooted in a combination of ego, conquest-driven instincts, or societal conditioning that normalizes or even romanticizes male infidelity. Men tend to experiment more—testing boundaries, chasing novelty, or seeking validation through multiple emotional or physical relationships. Yet, despite these repeated efforts, they often fail—not just in execution, but in emotional outcome.

More often than not, these pursuits leave them empty, misunderstood, or regretful. They may end up hurting someone, including themselves, and find themselves right back where they started—emotionally confused, longing for something real but unable to attain it through deception.

The tragedy lies in the repetition. Instead of learning from the experience, some men circle back to the same behaviour, seeking new opportunities to cheat or manipulate, unaware that what they're actually seeking is not conquest, but connection—something that cannot be achieved through dishonesty.

In the grand scheme, love tests both genders, but in different ways. For women, the challenge might be in choosing wisely and protecting their emotional space. For men, it's often about restraint, integrity, and recognizing that real love cannot be won through tricks or tested through betrayal. Eventually, life has a way of returning everyone to their emotional baseline—what you truly carry within. And no matter how far one strays in search of fleeting pleasures, the journey back to authenticity is the only path that brings peace.

As time passes, and as age and experience deepen, the man who tirelessly runs within the square of life begins to understand a quiet, unsettling truth: no matter how far he runs, no matter how many corners we turn, the end remains the same.

In the early stages of life, we run with passion—chasing dreams, success, recognition, love, and material comfort. With every milestone we reach, our hunger grows, and with it, so does our ambition. Driven by a natural and often unconscious desire for more, we begin to stretch the sides of our square—expanding its boundaries in pursuit of greater space, more possessions, wider influence, and constant validation.

As the square swells, it begins to shift—sometimes taking the form of a rectangle, sometimes dissolving into a shapeless track of endless striving. The symmetry fades, and the pursuit becomes perpetual.

Yet no matter how far we extend the lines of our lives, no matter how vast we make our personal or professional empires, we cannot escape the quiet precision of destiny's geometry. Eventually, the fast-paced runner slows down—only to stand at the edge of a small, rectangular trench: the final enclosure, six feet by three, carved into the earth.

There, in that silent resting place, our race ends—not in the boardrooms we once strived to enter, not on the stages we aspired to own, but in the embrace of soil and stillness.

We dissolve—not just in physical death, but into nature, memory, and the fading echoes of time.

The great irony is that while we were busy trying to make life bigger, life was gently urging us to go deeper. And in the end, all the striving, expansion, and accumulation lead back to a single, unshakable truth: we came with nothing, and we return the same way—leaving behind not the size of our achievements, but the shape of our living.

"Nature wants you to fail; but inspires you to live and win—Magada"

CONE:

Inner Journey from Base to Apex

Of all the topics I've explored, this one resisted me the most. It disturbed my thoughts, defied my attempts, and remained elusive, like a rebellious child refusing to return home. Ironically, I had often woven these very mathematical analogies into many of my speeches — fluidly, effortlessly — yet when I tried to mould them into written form, they wouldn't obey. Words, like numbers, have their own logic. But unlike equations, they also have moods.

In that moment of struggle, I remembered something Rekha—*my wife* once told me during a similar creative impasse. With a calmness only she possesses, she said, *'Leave those characters alone for a while. Don't force them. Let them wander. Let them believe they can exist without their creator. They will return. They always do — when they realize they can't find their way without you.'*

I followed her advice. I let go. I stopped commanding the story and gave it its space. I didn't write — not out of surrender, but out of respect for the process. And just as she predicted, they returned. Not just as words on a page, but as companions tugging at my sleeves, whispering truths, begging to be written. They needed me, as much as I needed them. What once resisted, now flowed — not because I conquered it, but because I waited with patience, and trusted the silence between the sentences.

Cone is the shape or design which has least surface area among all the structures. Now, I wonder, why these Vietnamese and other South Asian farmers wear the caps of this shape. It keeps their head coolest possible level compared to other shaped caps. Even in our lives, we have to take the shape of cone and follow its principles.

The Shape of Wisdom: Living Like a Cone

When I first noticed the Vietnamese farmers in the Mekong Delta wearing those distinct conical hats — the *nón lá* — I admired the elegance of their simplicity. These caps, woven from palm leaves, seemed too delicate to stand the test of hard labour under the tropical sun. But as I walked further along the paddies, I realized they weren't just hats. They were wisdom worn on the head — not by accident, but by deep tradition, knowledge, and unspoken engineering.

Later, in a quiet moment under a Banyan tree, a strange thought crept into my mind: *Why a cone?* Why not a dome or a wide-brimmed circle like the hats of cowboys, or even a square fabric like the Middle Eastern *keffiyeh*? Or flathead caps made of areca leaves in the coastal Karnataka. The answer wasn't just cultural — it was mathematical.

A cone, I recalled, has the minimum surface area for a given volume. In other words, it exposes the least of itself to the outside world while sheltering the most within. It lets the heat and harshness slide away, while creating a calm, cool space beneath. That's why their heads remained cooler in the burning sun — the design was not accidental. It was mindful, intentional, and humble.

And then, as always, philosophy began to whisper through science.

The Shape of Ego

In our youth, most of us want to be spheres — equal in all directions, showing every facet of ourselves. We stretch out our ambitions, inflate our presence, try to impress in every direction. Like balloons, we want to be noticed, even if it means exposing more of ourselves than necessary. Rather than becoming rich, we try to look like rich. But what does this actually gain us? More eyes watching us, more pressure, more surface to burn.

A sphere may seem perfect, but it's vulnerable. In life, those who expose too much often suffer the most heat.

The cone teaches restraint. It teaches purposeful direction. A cone doesn't spread itself everywhere. It narrows, focuses, points. And in that narrowing, it gains stability and direction. Cone does not have head to carry any load, but it has a stable base. *It doesn't try to be everything — it tries to be true to one thing.*

Isn't that what we need in life? To find a peak — a purpose — and align everything else around it? The cone is widest at the base — generous, grounded, inclusive. But it tapers toward a point, a focus, a *dharma*. It balances openness with intent.

Cooling the Mind

The farmers knew something many of us forget: the mind needs cooling. In a world of urgency, where every notification is a knock on our skull, we allow too much sunlight to reach our mental skin. We burn. We become irritated, restless, fatigued — not because of external pressure, but because we have no shape that protects us.

The cone — as a cap and as a metaphor — protects the most vital part: the head.

In life, too, we need a shield — a structure — to preserve clarity, thought, and perspective. We can't let everything in. We need filtration. We need form. And form follows function.

Think of the sage, the monk, the wise teacher. They live simply, dress minimally, speak only when needed.

They, too, wear an invisible cone — not of palm leaves, but of thought. They know how to reduce their surface area. They know that power doesn't come from broadcasting, but from channelling.

The Principle of Channelling

The cone has another secret: it channels energy. Flip it, and it becomes a funnel. The same structure that protects can also direct. This is not a coincidence.

The more focused your shape, the more powerful your flow. That's the principle of the cone. Be wide when it comes to receiving knowledge, but narrow when it comes to expressing action. Take in much. Do only what matters.

That's how rivers are born. They gather widely from hills, but carve valleys by narrowing their flow.

In our lives, we need this principle of reduction. Not everything needs our reaction. Not every argument needs our reply. Not every ambition needs chasing. The cone whispers to us: *Reduce. Refine. Reflect.*

Becoming the Cone

So, what does it mean to live like a cone? It means to ground yourself broadly — in values, in empathy, in learning. Let your base be wide, touching many lives. But let your identity taper toward clarity. Don't stay broad and scattered. Find your own peak. Know where your vertex is.

Your peak need not be fame or fortune. It could be wisdom. Peace. Service. Insight. Whatever it is, let your life point toward it.

And when the sun of the world scorches your soul with its demands, let your cone keep your head cool. Let it remind you: you don't have to do everything to matter. You just have to do one thing rightly.

That's why I think of the cone as the geometry of wisdom — and of humility. It saves energy, protects the core, and directs intent. It doesn't scream. It shelters.

Lessons from the Field

Back in the Mekong, I watched a farmer fix the frayed edge of his nón lá. He didn't throw it away. He mended it. That hat, humble and timeworn, was his shield, his shade, his signature.

I realized then: *we all carry invisible hats like that*. Some wear chaos, others ego, some wear ambition like a crown of thorns. But the wise — the quietly impactful — wear the cone.

Let us, too, shape our lives like a cone — grounded, cantered, cool-headed, and purposefully pointed.

The Triangle of Spiritual Energy

When we take the first step in imbibing spiritual wisdom and bringing positive changes in our lives, we learn that it is the soul that thinks, feels, perceives, and also speaks and performs actions through the physical body. Also, we learn about the Law of Karma, and God teaches us that actions based on soul consciousness, full of wisdom, qualities, and powers, are positive ones, and actions based on body consciousness, under the influence of negative personality traits, are negative ones. Soul empowerment takes place when we stop performing negative actions and start performing more positive actions.

We also need to remember God to increase our seven original virtues – peace, joy, love, bliss, purity, power, and wisdom. As the soul becomes more pure, positive, and powerful, we feel lighter, more stable, and very content. As we feel better, our faith in God and relationship with God become deeper, and we start connecting with God with more and more love and determination. Also, we experience more success in all the main spheres of our life – inner personality transformation, health, relationships, education, personal and professional roles, wealth, etc.

As our soul power increases, we feel the urge to share our spiritual benefits with others and we start telling them how meditation is useful and how beginning the day with practicing meditation and studying spiritual wisdom makes the entire day beautiful and fulfilling. When looking at this process, we compare it with a triangle.

Our self-connection with God represents one side of the triangle; others who benefit from our spiritual progress and learning represent another side of the triangle. As a result, others get connected with God, which represents the third side of the triangle. We can also see the 3 corners of the triangle as A being us, B being God, and C being others. Side AB represents our self-progress by connecting with God. Side AC represents our service of others and our effort to connect them with God, and side BC represents others' benefit with the help of their connection with God. This is the Triangle of Spiritual Energy and it represents the two most basic processes of spirituality – filling and sharing of spiritual treasures. This triangle makes our and others' lives beautiful and full of God's goodness and strength.

Faith and trust, though often intertwined, are distinct concepts rooted in different foundations. Faith typically involves a belief in the unseen or intangible, relying on spiritual conviction or acceptance without empirical evidence, such as having faith in a higher power or the inherent goodness of humanity. Trust, conversely, is built on experience and evidence, cultivated through consistent reliability—like trusting a friend to keep a promise based on their past actions.

While faith embraces uncertainty, often persisting even in doubt, trust depends on predictability and can erode if promises are broken. Both require vulnerability, yet faith leans into the unknown with hope, whereas trust is anchored in the familiarity of proven dependability.

Together, they shape how individuals navigate relationships, spirituality, and the uncertainties of life. However, this triangle is 3-dimensional which takes the shape of cone. Even in real life, our life gets tapered towards the top.

"Diamonds won’t emit light; they only reflect the light. Be the light—Magada"

The Diamond

Many find immense value in gold, platinum, diamonds, pearls, and sapphires. Strangely—or perhaps fortunately—I seem to be allergic to all such things. To me, they are no different from the pebbles that lie unnoticed on the ground. Their glitter holds no sway over me.

During my teaching days at the University of Agricultural Sciences, Bangalore, may in the year 2008, I noticed a student—incidentally, the son of a Member of the Legislative Assembly—seated in the middle row. What struck me wasn't his intellect or engagement, but a gleaming gold chain around his neck, proudly displayed through his open shirt buttons.

I invited him to the stage, not to scold but to awaken. I asked him to remove the chain and place it on the table. Though hesitant, he complied. I gently told him that such adornments were unnecessary in my classroom. "Instead," I said, "aspire to become gold yourself—pure, valuable, and rare by your own deeds."

The class burst into laughter. I added, "I don't wear gold, because I am the gold." Their laughter grew louder, but I remained still—because I meant it.

In my motivational talks, I often draw upon the elemental truth of carbon—a single substance that manifests in two vastly different forms: graphite and diamond. It is a powerful metaphor for life. The same carbon, when subjected to immense pressure and time, transforms from something ordinary into something extraordinary. I use this to illustrate a deeper truth: that greatness is not gifted, but forged—under stress, through resilience, and by embracing risk.

Yet, there is a lesser-known truth about diamonds that often goes unnoticed. Despite their clarity and value, diamonds do not emit light of their own. They merely reflect what is cast upon them. In darkness, they lose their glory; without light, they are no different than a polished stone.

And so, I remind my audience: becoming a diamond is not the end. Seek not just to reflect brilliance, but to become a source of it. Let your inner light—of wisdom, purpose, and compassion—shine so that even in the absence of external glow, you still illuminate the world.

Fishermen and the Diamond

On the rugged edge of the world where the land meets the sea, a lone fisherman awoke in the stillness of the night.

It was just 3:00 a.m.—a time when the stars still linger in the sky, unwilling to surrender to the dawn. While the rest of the village slept wrapped in the warmth of dreams, he rose with purpose, guided not by clocks, but by an ancient rhythm woven into his blood through generations.

Fishermen, by tradition, are early risers. But this man, weathered by wind and wave, rose even earlier—not out of anxiety, but reverence. He stepped barefoot onto the cold earth and walked to the shore, where the sea meets stone in a quiet, ageless conversation.

The beach was cloaked in darkness so complete it felt like a blanket stitched by the cosmos itself. The casuarina trees stood tall like silent monks in meditation, and yet, they whispered—a sharp, hissing hymn carried by the cold wind. Each strong wind cut through the night like a sharp knife, but it brought no harm—only carried the weight of the deep darkness.

Waves rose from the depths and crashed against the ancient rocks with mighty force, only to retreat back into stillness. There was a rhythm in their violence—an ebb and flow that echoed life itself: the rise of passion, the fall into peace. Between these crashes, a strange calmness emerged—a silence so profound that even the wind respected it.

Despite the chaotic symphony of nature—the roar of waves, the hiss of wind, the crackle of leaves—there was peace. A stillness so deep it echoed within the soul. In that moment, the night wasn't dark—it was infinite. Not silent, but sacred.

This wasn't just a man going fishing. This was a man stepping into the arms of the universe, seeking not just fish, but clarity. In his solitude, he wasn't alone. He was part of something vast and eternal—like the sea, the wind, and the darkness itself.

Before dawn's first whisper, the fisherman climbed a jagged outcrop and settled there to wait for enough light to push his boat to sea. Loneliness has its own small rituals: some chew their nails, others hum to break the silence. He discovered a handful of small stones at his side and, half-absent, began pitching them into the black water—each one leaving behind a soft, hollow *plunk … plunk … plunk*. The act became a rhythm, a pulse that filled the night as the hours drifted by unnoticed.

When the horizon finally blushed with morning and the sky turned pearl-grey, he rose to ready his nets. A twinge of curiosity he wanted to know what exactly had he been throwing away? He glanced down and found only no single stone left. He had one last stone in his hands. In the new-born light it caught a fierce gleam; it was no stone at all, but a flawless diamond. A cold wave of realization swept over him: all night long he had been idly flinging precious gems into the sea, mistaking them for worthless pebbles simply because darkness had hidden their nature.

Shock gave way to sorrow—fortune squandered by the hand that never knew what it held. Yet the diamond itself offered a final lesson: value is invisible until light unveils it. So it is with human life. If we spend our nights of ignorance chasing glitter we cannot see, we may discard what is priceless within us. It could be our health, our peace of mind, or our true happiness—we often sacrifice these in the pursuit of big dreams. We chase success with relentless determination, believing that reaching the top will bring fulfilment. And yes, many do achieve what they set out for—wealth, status, recognition. But often, once they reach that long-sought destination, a quiet realization dawns: the price they paid was too high.

What seemed like success begins to feel hollow when they look back and see what they lost along the way—precious time with loved ones, their physical or mental well-being, or the simple joys of life. Only then do they understand that success is not just about reaching the goal; it's also about how we get there, and what we carry—or leave behind—on the journey. Not all victories are worth the cost.

Better to become diamond than to clutch at diamonds; better to seek the light of understanding than to mourn what was lost in the dark.

Position your spirit, then, as a finely cut gem—angled toward wisdom's radiance. When you catch that light, do not hoard it; reflect it outward to shatter the world's shadows and darkness. What matters is not how many jewels we gather, but how brightly we can shine—revealing, by our own clarity, the hidden worth in everything and everyone around us.

Human life is not just a biological event—it is a sacred gift, a divine opportunity wrapped in time. Life itself is a masterpiece of the universe, crafted with moments of contentment, joy, wonder, and purpose. It is designed not merely to be endured but to be celebrated, cherished, and lived with awareness.

Yet, so many people forget this truth. They become prisoners of their own egos, trapped in the silos of pride, comparison, and endless ambition. In their pursuit of more—more wealth, more recognition, more control—they neglect the treasures already present: family, friendship, laughter, silence, sunrise, and breath. They live disconnected, as if life is a race rather than a rhythm. And only when death looms near—when time seems to run out—do they begin to understand what truly mattered all along.

So, after you read this chapter, don't rush. Close the book. Lay down. Rest. Let your mind breathe. When you wake up tomorrow, open your eyes as if seeing the world for the very first time. Look around—not with judgment, but with awe. Appreciate the warmth of the morning light, the sound of birds, the smile of a loved one, the blessing of your body moving with ease. Begin to notice, begin to feel, begin to live.

Because the world hasn't changed—but your awareness has. And that, perhaps, is the greatest miracle of life: when we begin to see, we begin to live.

"Nature wants you to fail; but inspires you to live and win—Magada"

Zen and a Naked Women

Long ago, in a land where mountains rose like silent prayers and rivers whispered through ancient trees, there lived a Zen master. He had no possessions to call his own—only a wooden bowl, a faded robe, and the vast, calm ocean of his mind.

One quiet morning, the Zen master set out on a journey through the forest. With him walked eight disciples, each clad in simple robes, their eyes lowered not out of shame but reverence. They were not seeking a temple built of stone—they were searching for a space where the world fell away, and only truth remained.

They walked in silence, their footsteps pressing gently into the damp earth, as if not to disturb the dreams of the forest. The trail led them upstream, against the current—both of water and of life. They moved slowly, not out of tiredness, but because each step was a meditation.

As the sky began to blush with the colours of dawn, they arrived at a clearing nestled beside a flowing stream. The forest there was alive but not noisy. The casuarina trees stood tall, swaying in rhythm with the wind, their needle-like leaves making a soft hissing song. The water splashed over pebbles, smooth and musical. The scent of wildflowers hung in the air, mixing with the earthy perfume of peat soil.

The Weight We Carry

The forest path twisted gently, and the morning mist curled like incense through the trees. A Zen master and his eight disciples were walking along the riverbank, in search of a quiet place to settle and meditate. Their robes were plain, their minds trained in detachment, and their hearts tuned to the silence of the world.

As they approached a shallow but rushing river, a sudden figure emerged from the mist—a woman, completely unclothed, standing helpless by the river's edge.

She bowed and, with visible desperation, pleaded, "Please, help me cross this river."

The disciples froze. Their teachings echoed in their minds: detachment from desire, separation from worldly entanglements, especially from the allure of the flesh. To them, her presence was not just surprising—it was a test.

Each monk turned his gaze away, retreating inward, refusing silently. Yet the Zen master stepped forward without hesitation. With a calm face and steady hands, he gently lifted the woman onto his shoulders, crossed the river, and set her down on the other side. She thanked him with folded hands and disappeared into the forest path.

The disciples were stunned.

They followed in silence, too bound by reverence and confusion to speak. Hours passed. They walked through bamboo groves, forded small streams, and finally stopped in a serene clearing to set up camp.

Evening descended. The rituals were performed—the tents raised, wild fruits collected, and firewood stacked. Yet peace eluded them. The master, as always, settled into his meditation. But the minds of his disciples were far from still. The image of their guru carrying the naked woman burned in their thoughts.

Finally, unable to hold back any longer, the youngest among them mustered the courage to speak. The others joined him, their voices trembling more from inner conflict than fear.

"Master," they asked, "we are taught to be free from desire, to avoid even the shadow of attachment. Yet today, you carried a naked woman across the river. How could you, a teacher of detachment, do that?"

The master opened his eyes slowly. A faint smile crossed his face—not of mockery, but of deep understanding.

He walked to a nearby stone, sat with effortless grace, and closed his eyes again.

Then, he spoke softly, as if speaking to the wind.

"I left her at the riverbank… Why are you still carrying her?"

And with that, he drifted into deep meditation.

The story is not about a river or a woman—it is about the mind. We often claim to walk the path of detachment, yet we carry burdens not in our hands, but in our thoughts. The master's action was one of compassion, untouched by desire, free from judgment. He responded to a human need and moved on.

But the disciples, though outwardly detached, clung to the memory—attached to the idea of what "should" and "should not" be.

In life, too, we carry many such "naked women" in our minds—moments, judgments, past events, imagined wrongs. They weigh us down far more than any physical load. True detachment is not avoidance—it is the ability to act with clarity and leave no trace of ego behind. The lesson is simple, yet profound: Let go of what no longer walks beside you.

Hours passed.

No one moved.

No one needed to.

Because here, in this untouched patch of earth, nothing was missing. There was no talk of ambitions, no weight of past or future—only the sacred pulse of the present moment. For the Zen, this journey was not a break from life—it was life. They had not come here to escape the world, but to remember how to be part of it again. As the sun climbed the sky and birds flew above, not a word had been spoken. But in that silence, everything had been said.

"Nature aligns itself with those who dare to dream big—Magada"

Weaver Bird

I have often found myself pondering a fundamental question: Why is it that in almost all species, it is the male that seems to dominate—physically, socially, and sometimes even symbolically? This question lingered in my mind for years, echoing through the corridors of observation, culture, and even science. I searched for answers not just in society but in nature itself—until one fine day, over three decades ago, life gently offered me a window.

It was in the year 1992 that I stumbled upon a profound book titled *The Nature of Life*, authored by Janet and Hopson. But the story of how I came upon it is, in itself, quite fascinating.

There was a ship called 'Doulos', a floating library of sorts, that travelled across continents carrying millions of books—a sea-bound sanctuary of knowledge. When this ship docked at the Mangalore Port, the opportunity felt almost divine. I went there with a few close friends, drawn more by curiosity than by intent. But what I found aboard changed me.

The ship didn't sell books for profit. Instead, they charged only for transportation—as if to say, knowledge has no price, but sharing it has a small cost. Among the ocean of titles, my eyes caught the glimmer of *The Nature of Life*. It was priced at a steep Rs. 35,000, an amount far beyond my reach at that time. Yet, to my disbelief, I was told I could take it home for just Rs. 750.

I held the book as if it were a sacred scroll, heavy not in weight but in wisdom.

In that book, nestled among insights drawn from biology, evolution, and ethology, I found my answer—not just to the question of male dominance, but to many subtle dynamics of life itself. It unfolded the layered roles of gender in nature, illustrating that what we often perceive as dominance is merely a surface phenomenon, shaped by evolutionary roles, environmental necessities, and reproductive strategies.

It taught me that true power is not always loud—that femininity, often silent and overlooked in the wild, is just as crucial, potent, and foundational as masculinity. It reminded me that nature itself does not favour ego; it favours balance.

That small book, picked up from a giant ship, became one of the greatest teachers in my life.

Darwin's Statement

Charles Darwin expressed the idea that "Males compete and females choose" in his influential book "The Descent of Man, and Selection in Relation to Sex" (1871). In this book, Darwin introduced the concept of sexual selection, a form of natural selection. He argued that:

- **Males of many species often compete** with one another for access to females (through displays, combat, or other means).
- **Females, in turn, tend to choose** among the competing males based on certain traits (such as bright colours, elaborate songs, or strength), because these traits may signal genetic fitness.

While Darwin did not use the exact modern phrasing "males compete, females choose", this principle is a simplified summary of his sexual selection theory.

I extended my thinking while reading 'The Nature of Life' where I came across the selection process in Weaver birds. The Weaver bird, found mainly in sub-Saharan Africa and parts of Asia, is best known for its extraordinary nest-building skills. The male of the species weaves complex and beautiful nests—hanging globes, tunnels, or baskets—using grass, twigs, and palm strips to attract a mate. The nest isn't just a shelter; it is a symbol of creativity, patience, effort, and devotion. Females do not know how to build these complex nests.

Normally, hundreds of birds find a river bank or wetlands and build the nests at the tip of a hanging branch particularly towards the water. It is to avoid the predators. Because of the changing ecosystem and human intervention in all possible areas, we find stray number of hanging nests in unusual places.

The weaving is an engineering marvellous, even a textile engineers cannot understand its complex weaving design. At first glance, it looks like a wild tuft of grass swinging from a branch, no different from a loose cluster of leaves blown together by the wind. But look closer—and linger long enough—and you'll see something astonishing.

There, in the gentle sway of a tropical breeze, hangs a nest so intricate, so methodically constructed, that even the finest architects would nod in reverence. It is the work of the Weaver bird, the unassuming artist of the skies.

From the moment the male weaver selects a pliable strand of grass, he becomes a craftsman, an engineer, a sculptor—and perhaps, most profoundly, a poet. With nothing more than his beak and instinct passed down from generations, he begins his labour.

He starts with a single knot. Yes, a knot—woven with beak and claw, twisted around a slender branch. It's his foundation, his first verse. From here, the nest grows—a spherical chamber, suspended like a lantern. He works tirelessly, hour after hour, weaving each blade of grass over and under, curling it in calculated loops, binding it tightly without glue, nails, or plans drawn on paper.

Some nests have a long entrance tunnel, pointing downward like the throat of a pitcher. This is no decorative flourish. It's a defense—a narrow passage that wards off snakes and other intruders, allowing only the small-bodied weaver to slip in. Inside, the nest is surprisingly spacious. The inner chamber is lined with soft grasses, forming a cradle of calm where eggs will eventually rest, warmed by the breast of a female—if she deems it worthy.

Yes, this elaborate creation is not guaranteed to be accepted. The female comes, inspects, judges. Sometimes she flies away, unimpressed. If she does, the male does not plead. He simply tears down his nest, strand by strand, and begins again—not in despair, but in devotion. its nest is not only shelter but signature, not just architecture but audition. It is built with precision, urgency, and silent hope.

Firefly Lanterns: The Weavers of Light and Clay

After days—sometimes weeks—of relentless labour under the sun and amidst the whispers of wind, the Weaver bird completes what is perhaps one of nature's finest dwellings. But its work does not end with mere construction. No, for this small bird is not only an architect but an artist with a flair for illumination.

When the woven fortress is strong, aerodynamic, and secure, the weaver bird begins the final phase—embellishment with elements of the earth and sky. From the edges of muddy shores or damp riverbanks, it collects soft, wet clay, carefully carrying small globules in its beak. These are not just random touches. They are strategic daubs of earthen texture, applied thoughtfully around the nest, possibly to strengthen or balance, or perhaps... to prepare a canvas for what comes next.

What happens afterward is both mesmerizing and poetic—they catch fireflies.

Yes, the weaver birds, with all their silent wisdom, gently capture fireflies and affix them onto the damp clay patches. The sticky mud holds these bioluminescent guests like nature's glue, and the fireflies, still glowing softly, become living lamps. Their gentle greenish-gold light begins to shimmer in the night, turning a simple nest into a glowing lantern of life.

One can imagine the riverside under the velvet sky, lined with hundreds of such nests, each swaying gently in the evening breeze, adorned with flickering fireflies. It is not unlike our own traditions—when we decorate our newly built homes with strings of lights, celebrating achievement, protection, and the joy of living.

But these weaver birds do it not for ceremony, but for instinct, beauty, and perhaps, courtship—a soft signal to their partners and to the world: "Here is a home, glowing with life, made with devotion."

The Architecture of Love: A Weaver's Courtship Ritual

In the secret world of weaver birds, where life is built strand by strand, a quiet ritual unfolds—one that mirrors the profound principles of selection, diligence, and worthiness. Once the male weaver completes his intricate masterpiece—woven with care, engineering precision, and instinctive beauty—he awaits not applause but evaluation. And it is not by chance or sympathy that his work is judged, but by a panel of perfectionists: the discerning female weavers.

These female birds, nature's most meticulous architects and critics, arrive in flocks and begin their assessment. Their examination is not casual; it is a dance of intention and scrutiny.

They randomly choose nests from the clusters hanging like ornaments along trees. They enter a few, one by one, and test every detail:

- The thickness of the walls—for insulation and strength.
- The height and depth—for safety from predators.

- The clever false entrance—a deceptive design to mislead the cunning eyes of snakes or raptors.

Inside, the females bounce and jerk the nest deliberately, much like a mother checking a cradle, to ensure its grip on the branch is steadfast. They want to know: *Can this shelter endure the howling winds and the tempestuous rains?* Will it protect future life?

And still not done, they fly out and circle back, hurling themselves at the nests with controlled force, beating them with their wings. It is not aggression—it is a final test of strength, ensuring the knots that hold the nest are woven not just by fibre, but with foresight and fortitude.

This is nature's audition for fatherhood—no words, no promises—only skill, patience, and resilience are measured.

Among many, one nest might pass the trials. The female then lingers longer. She pauses—not out of fatigue, but because she has chosen. And this lingering is a signal. The male, watching silently from nearby, understands her gesture. He enters the nest with her. There begins their union—the creation of a family, a shared life nurtured within the threads of craftsmanship and choice.

This ritual, seemingly simple to the onlooker, is a profound reflection of natural selection. Here, beauty alone does not win; it is the marriage of utility and strength, design and endurance, that earns the right to nurture new life. In the tale of the weavers lies a message for us all:

- Not everything that is beautiful is chosen.
- It is the structure that withstands pressure, the design that defies chaos, and the foundation that survives scrutiny—that earns trust.
- In both nature and life, acceptance comes not from attraction alone, but from the depth of effort and purpose.

So, the next time you see a weaver's nest swinging gently in the breeze, remember: it is not merely a nest—it is a silent testament to patience, excellence, and worthiness—a love letter written in grass and tested by the wind. In the quiet wisdom of nature, the message is clear — the finest nest, built with strength and purpose, is chosen by the most discerning of hearts. Thus, strength seeks grace, and grace rewards strength.

The behaviour of the weaver bird reveals a profound truth about life and nature's strategy. Across most life forms where there exists a distinction between sexes, nature has bestowed the power of choice upon the female, while the male must compete—proving his worth through strength, skill, or beauty. Only in human society does it *appear* that the male is the one who chooses. In truth, however, he is simply engaged in an endless pursuit to exhibit what society deems as strength—status, wealth, knowledge, or charm—so that the woman, the true chooser, may consider him worthy.

If a woman decides to fall in love, she holds within her the quiet power to draw the attention of many suitors—even within a single day. Her willingness, her choice, and her openness can open doors effortlessly. For men, however, the journey is often quite different. He must strive—sometimes for months or even years—to express, impress, and convince the one he admires.

This is not merely about charm or appearance—it reflects the deeper design of nature. In most species, the female is the one who chooses, and the male performs. He must sing the loudest song, build the safest nest, or battle the strongest rival—all to prove he is worthy. The same truth echoes in human love. A woman's simple 'yes' has immense power. It can change lives. Yet she rarely says it lightly, for her heart is not easily swayed by words alone—it listens for sincerity, steadiness, and strength. Love, in this way, is not a conquest but a calling. And the one who chooses holds the sacred right to set its terms.

I allowed my thoughts to dive deeper into the mystery of natural selection, hoping to grasp more fully the underlying wisdom that governs life itself. And in that contemplation, a profound realization dawned on me: nature is not just functional—it is flawlessly intentional.

At its very core, the purpose of life in all species is remarkably simple—**to live and to reproduce**. The act of living, though not without struggle, is something most of the 7.8 billion people on this planet manage in some way. We find food, shelter, companionship, a place in society. That is survival. But reproduction—that is an entirely different challenge. It is not merely a biological act but an investment of trust, energy, and life itself, especially for the female of the species.

In nature's grand design, the burden and the beauty of reproduction lie disproportionately with the female. While the male may contribute a moment of genetic material, the female offers everything—her blood, her flesh, her time, her peace, and even, potentially, her life. In the process of creating new life, she may endure unbearable pain. Indeed, labour pain is considered one of the greatest known to humanity—a pain so profound that even one woman cannot fully explain it to another.

And so, nature—wise, just, and purposeful—has bestowed upon the female the sovereign right to choose. It is not about fairness; it is about survival. Since she bears the cost, she deserves the choice. Nature ensures that she selects not just any mate, but the one who shows strength, resilience, adaptability—traits that may give her offspring the best chance at enduring the hardships of an unpredictable world.

This selection process, sometimes subtle and instinctive, is a genetic filtration system, a silent ritual that ensures the continuation of strong lineages. The male must compete, must prove, must become worthy—not for dominance, but for acceptance.

In the end, nature teaches us this: **the one who carries the future deserves the power to choose it.**

After reading this story, take a moment—not just to admire it, but to reflect. Go back within yourself. Dig deep and discover your core strength—that one quality, skill, or value that sets you apart. Each of us is born with a unique spark, but we often spend our lives chasing borrowed lights instead of nurturing our own flame.

Whatever field you choose—be it art, science, service, entrepreneurship, or simply living with grace—commit to it with depth, clarity, and passion. Mastery is not about fame; it is about alignment. When your inner strength aligns with your chosen path, excellence becomes inevitable.

And then, something magical happens: you stop chasing admiration—instead, you attract it. The very energy you once sought from others will begin to flow toward you. You won't be striving for someone's attention; the world will pause and take notice.

Why seek validation from one person, one moment, or one love, when you have the potential to inspire an entire world? Be so exceptional, so deeply rooted in your purpose, that your life becomes a lighthouse for others—visible, unwavering, and needed.

Let the story be a mirror, not just a tale. Look into it—and rise.

" Grammar has no single author—only compilers. In life, be the author and write your own grammar —Magada"

Beauty and the King

The dynasty had been inherited—not earned. It came to him wrapped in the silk of privilege, soaked in the blood of past warriors, and seated atop a throne that was once built with purpose, vision, and sacrifice. But by the time King Sampath—a name that ironically meant "Wealth"—ascended to power, all that remained of the empire's dignity was its golden sheen. Like many rulers born into luxury, he inherited the palace but not the purpose.

His rule bore no mission, his governance had no direction. He was not a leader but a consumer—consuming pleasures, lands, and people without pause. Instead of expanding boundaries or elevating culture, he made compromises with powerful neighbouring dynasties, surrendering independence in exchange for opulence. To maintain the illusion of power, he paid tributes and signed agreements—pacts not of peace but of convenience. He ruled, not with the fire of vision, but with the smoke of self-indulgence.

Lust was his court's anthem. The king's appetite for pleasure knew no end. The moment his eyes caught beauty, it was summoned. The court became a marketplace of flesh, and dignity was bartered in whispers. There were men—drunk on the dream of gold—who offered their virgin daughters at the altar of greed, hoping to buy favour, land, or wealth in return. Morality was twisted until it resembled duty, and silence became a tradition in the corridors of power.

The king believed he owned everything—even innocence. And like many tyrants of history, he confused ownership with love, possession with power, and indulgence with immortality. But history, ever the patient observer, watches silently. Kings like Sampath leave behind no monuments of virtue, only ruins soaked in the sighs of forgotten lives.

This tale is not just a historical reflection, but a mirror to the ongoing human condition. Lust and greed have not vanished; they merely wear modern masks—of status, luxury, and influence. The message is timeless: when power loses its purpose, it becomes a playground for corruption. When a joker become a king, the King's court becomes a 'Circus.'

The Wealth Chasing Beauty

King Sampath, though far from a skilled hunter, often ventured into the wilderness under the guise of hunting. In truth, it was not the thrill of pursuit nor the ethics of the hunt that drew him—it was the illusion of dominion, the power to take life at will, and the intoxicating arrogance of being feared by the wild itself. Surrounded by his loyal guards and draped in royal leisure, he would point at animals like a child at toys, while his soldiers identified the prey and placed the bow in his hand. He would release the arrow—often missing the mark, but no one dared to mention it.

It was on one such hollow expedition that fate intervened.

Amidst the dense green, where the sun pierced through the canopy in golden slivers, a soldier caught sight—not of a beast, but of a girl. Her name was Sundari, meaning "the beautiful girl." She was not adorned in jewels nor dressed in silks, but her natural elegance outshone every gem in the king's treasury. She was a woodcutter—humble, rugged, and rooted in the earth—living on the fringe of the forest that bordered the king's opulent world.

When the king's eyes met her silhouette between the trees, he lost interest in the hunt. The wilderness that once trembled at his presence now faded before a single silent girl. He stopped his chariot. His hands, once eager to pull the bow, now clenched with desire of another kind.

That evening, in his private court hall, he gave an order—not for her admiration, but for her submission. A soldier was dispatched with instructions: by the next sunset, the girl should bathe, dress finely, and arrive discreetly through the rear gate of the palace. It was not an invitation; it was an imperial command.

But Sundari did not bend. She neither trembled nor flattered. She heard the messenger, looked at the axe in her hand, and returned to her pile of wood. She had no place for palaces in her heart, and no hunger for golden illusions. She refused. Quietly. Completely.

The soldiers returned, laughing at her audacity. "How can beauty turn her back on Sampath, the King of Wealth?" they mocked. But the king was not amused. For the first time in his life, he had been denied. Not by an army. Not by a storm. But by a girl with no armour, no status, and no fear.

Humiliation crept into his royal veins. His ego burned with the salt of rejection. His instinct cried for revenge—a command, a sword, a death. But something within restrained him. Perhaps it was wonder. Perhaps it was an unfamiliar recognition of something sacred—a spirit unbought, a will untouched.

He let her live. Not out of mercy, but out of mystery. He needed to know: What gave her such power to say no to a king? And so, with minds unsettled and hearts shaken, the hunting party turned back—not with trophies, but with questions.

The 'Fame' Chasing the Beauty

The matter went viral in the town. People started speaking about the Sundari rejecting the king. The new tales started sprawling. People even surprised to know that she was not punished and started admiring her boldly. The 'Keerthi'- meaning 'Famous', a court hall singer who was famous among many dynasties known for his singing excellence and the smartness came to know that an ordinary girl rejected the king.

He was never far from the king's shadow. In wealth, indulgence, and self-admiration, he walked stride for stride with royalty. Sri Sri Sri Pandit Keerthi, the court's most revered singer, was not merely a man of music but a man intoxicated by his own fame. His pride was not rooted in his voice alone—it was in the adoration he commanded, the tales of love spun around him from palace to palace. He believed he was a melody no woman could refuse.

With that ego echoing in his heart, he set out toward the forest, accompanied by his entourage. This time, however, he carried no song—only a purpose. To summon the girl who had dared to reject the king himself. Never in the history of their opulent dynasty had a man of such status gone into the wild to invite a woman. It was always the other way around. In their world, rejection was a myth, something that happened to ordinary men—not to kings or to Keerthi.

As they reached the humble hut nestled in the trees, one of the soldiers stepped forward, calling toward the doorway. He cleared his throat and declared with pomp, "The great Asthana Gayaka, the court's celestial voice—Sri Sri Sri Pandit Keerthi—has come to meet you."

Inside the hut, Sundari heard the name. She understood the weight it carried, the cultural currents that surrounded it, the prestige soaked in his titles. But she did not tremble. She neither rushed nor rose. She simply continued with her task—cutting, sorting, living. Her silence was louder than their drums. She knew their world, their pride, their vanity—and she chose not to be part of it.

For Keerthi and his men, it was an unfamiliar silence. A silence that did not revere, did not fear, and did not yield. They all went back to the court with humiliation and shame.

The king, once draped in pride and unquestioned authority, now found himself unsettled by an unfamiliar feeling—rejection. The silence of Sundari echoed louder in his mind than the praises of a thousand courtiers. Her refusal had pierced his royal ego, not with a sword but with a silence he could not command.

What began as a flicker of insult slowly turned into a storm of anxiety. He, who was adored without question, now sat in his grand court, haunted by a forest girl's indifference. Many in the palace whispered in fear that Sundari's fate would be grim—that she might be publicly executed, hung from the city gates, or trampled under the feet of royal elephants, a spectacle used for centuries to instil obedience through terror.

But none of that came to pass.

Instead, the king did something unexpected—he chose restraint over rage, curiosity over cruelty. He summoned his wisest ministers, astrologers, and spies to deliberate. Their collective advice led to a different strategy. If a girl like Sundari could refuse the might of a monarch, perhaps she was not just an ordinary wood-seller. Perhaps there was a hidden reason, a secret, a forbidden love that gave her such courage.

And so, quietly, without a whisper to the world, the king commissioned a team of spies. Their mission was delicate yet urgent: to shadow Sundari from dawn to dusk, to watch her every step in the forest, to decode her silences, and most of all—to find out whom she truly loved, for in that answer, the king hoped to reclaim his wounded pride.

But what the spies were yet to realize was this: sometimes love isn't for someone, but for oneself, and true freedom cannot be traced through footsteps.

However, after few weeks, they collected her movements and daily routines. They found that she has fallen in love with an another wood seller who is a "Dumb Man." But, he is tall and handsome with a great physique.

When the king received the report, he sat in stunned disbelief. Sundari, the girl who had shaken the throne with a single refusal, was in love—not with a warrior, a nobleman, or a learned sage—but with a mere woodcutter. And not just any woodcutter—a man who was mute, without words, without wealth, and without stature.

The news struck the king like thunder rolling through a silent temple. His pride, carefully built over years of conquest and courtly praise, began to crumble under the weight of her simple choice. He had always believed that power could command desire, that women were drawn to strength, gold, and glory. But Sundari had chosen otherwise. She had chosen a man who could not speak, but perhaps spoke louder through silence than the king ever could with his decrees.

Humiliation engulfed the king like a wildfire. He ceased attending to matters of the state—the defense strategies, enemy intrusions, the famine crippling his borders, the rising unrest among his subjects. Nothing mattered. His world, once vast and governed by his command, had shrunk to the thought of one village girl and her impossible affection.

He abandoned the royal bedchambers, unable to touch his queens, unable even to feign interest in their presence. Sleep evaded him like a fugitive. Her face, her defiance, her silence—haunted his dreams and ruled his waking moments. The more he tried to push her out of his mind, the more vivid her presence became. Her rejection turned into an obsession, a fire that logic could not extinguish.

He was no longer the king of his kingdom. He had become a prisoner of his own unfulfilled desire. Madness crept in—not the madness of noise, but the madness of longing. Not for her body, but for the power to understand why she had not bowed. And that unanswered question became the most dangerous enemy he had ever faced.

One day, in a moment of rare clarity—perhaps born from sleepless nights or the humility that only unrequited love can teach—the king made a profound decision. He would not conquer love; he would honour it.

He issued a royal invitation to every corner of the kingdom, summoning nobles and commoners alike to the grand ceremonial grounds adjacent to the palace. It was not a declaration of war, nor a coronation of a prince. It was a celebration of something far more powerful—the union of two souls bound not by power or pedigree, but by choice and quiet devotion.

He called upon Sundari and the man she loved—a humble woodcutter, mute but radiant with truth. With regal dignity, he ordered that their wedding be conducted with all the splendour usually reserved for kings and queens, princes and princesses. The finest fabrics adorned them, musicians played celestial melodies, and the whole court shimmered with a light that felt less like luxury and more like liberation.

As Sundari and her beloved walked into the grand hall, dressed not as peasants but as royalty, the crowd erupted into an applause so thunderous that it echoed through the mountains and the pages of history. It was not merely the sound of celebration—it was the sound of awakening. The dancing, the feasting, the joy that unfolded that day had no precedent in the king's lineage.

Amid the jubilance, a minister leaning toward the king whispered, half in jest, "If women begin choosing their own men, half the men in the kingdom will be left with no purpose."

The king, still watching the couple with deep introspection, raised his hand and interrupted, "Stop. Do not speak a truth, I am still learning to accept."

He stood, majestic yet humble, and addressed the crowd. Silence fell like a sacred curtain.

> *"It is not about what men want. The true question is—do we have the courage to understand what women desire? For centuries, we have tried to possess love. But love is not a thing to be owned. It is a sacred fire that must be won with respect and understanding. If you truly wish to rule a heart, do not demand it—deserve it."*

Today, to send a message across time and kingdoms, I declare—Sundari shall be the new sovereign of this land. Let the world know that love cannot be silenced, and the freedom to choose is the first step toward a just world."

And as he spoke, the heavens themselves seemed to celebrate. The applause that followed was not merely for a marriage or a decree—it was for a kingdom that had awakened to the wisdom of the heart.

"Now, you read the earlier story again"

"There are three sides for truth. Your side, my side and the right side—
Magada"

Thamassu-
The Mental Darkness

[Scene Opens – Soft instrumental music fades out, and a warm spotlight centres on a minimalist stage.]

The curtain rises slowly.

Centre stage is a modest wooden table—slightly aged, with two sturdy chairs placed directly opposite each other. On the table rest two crystal glasses, each filled halfway with an amber liquid that glistens under the stage lights. The setting is quiet—charged with unspoken tension and hope.

From stage left, enters Mr. Shankara—an elderly man draped in a simple dhoti and a shawl over his shoulder. His forehead bears a prominent tilak, his gait composed yet firm. There is discipline in his movements, and reverence in his eyes.

From stage right, appears Mr. Mohammed—a middle-aged man, modestly dressed in a kurta and skullcap. His walk is calm, reflective. His eyes reveal both the wisdom of age and a trace of worldly sorrow.

They approach the table in silence, acknowledging each other with a slight bow of the head—not out of ritual, but respect.

They sit down gently, facing one another. The air between them is not heavy with animosity, but rather filled with the weight of history, expectation, and possibility.

A moment of stillness.

Each man slowly reaches for the glass in front of him. They lift it halfway to their lips—then pause. Their eyes meet. Something unspoken passes between them—a question, perhaps a doubt, maybe even an invitation to understanding.

They lower their glasses. A long breath. Then, with deliberate motion, they slide their glasses across the table, offering their drink to the other.

Each man now holds the other's glass.

Once again, they raise the glasses to drink.

And again—they stop.

Their hands tremble slightly, not from fear, but from the sheer magnitude of the gesture. This is no ordinary drink. This is the essence of the other. It represents culture, belief, ancestry—and also trust.

They set the glasses down again.

A long silence.

Then, without a word, both men reach forward and gently touch the rims of the two glasses together—like a silent toast. It is not about drinking now—it is about breaking the barrier.

A soft light glows above them, and the stage dims into twilight and brightens up again. The conversation goes like this,

Shankara: (looking down at the table, voice heavy with emotion) "Mohammed bhai… there's someone in my life I can't stand. My heart burns whenever I think of him. Tell me… what should I do with my enemy?"

Mohammed: (leaning back, half-smiling, eyes narrowing): "Simple. Finish him off. Kill the bastard. What else does an enemy deserve?"

[He chuckles bitterly, then pauses—his expression turning contemplative. He looks directly into Shankara's eyes.]

Mohammed: (softly) "But tell me, Shankara bhai… I too have an enemy. What do you think I should do?"

Shankara: (sighs, nods slowly, eyes darkening) "The same, Mohammed bhai. What's the point of letting him live? Kill him. End it once and for all."

[Suddenly—BOOM! A deafening gunshot echoes across the stage. The entire stage goes BLACKOUT.]

[Few seconds of silence. Audience holds their breath.]

[Slowly, a dim, cold light returns to the stage. Both men are slumped over the table, motionless. Blood on their shirts. The glasses have fallen. The silence is overwhelming.]

Narrator's Voice (off-stage, calm yet haunting):

"Hatred asks for blood.
Revenge knows no direction.
When you see an enemy in the mirror,
The bullet finds both hearts.
Two men. Two questions.
One answer.
And yet, no victor."

Narrator (voice calm, reflective, resonating in the silence):

"This is not just a story of two individuals.
They were called friends, yet they were poor at friendship.

They shared space, language, laughter—but not trust.
You may see this tale repeat itself—between people,
between families, among communities, across borders,
and through the very veins of nations.

In the end, they pointed their weapons not just at each other,
but at a shared past, misunderstood hearts, and unresolved wounds.
They pulled the trigger together.
Both fell.
But sometimes, only one does.
And the one who survives writes the next chapter.
We call him 'leader.'
He decides.
We watch.
And history keeps watching us—forever."

(Pauses. Then continues with deeper resonance.)

"When centuries of silence, suspicion, and separation
finally sit face to face,
even that silence becomes sacred—
a dialogue without words,
yet louder than screams.

And if there is to be peace—real peace—
It must rise from love:
Love for people.
Love for society.

Love for the Divine.
Because the heart that holds love
cannot hold a trigger."

[Lights fade. Curtain falls.]

"A snake, even if it is not poisonous, should pretend to be venomous — Chanakya"

The Snake and its Venom

"Everything in nature is food—it is the dose that makes the poison."

This ancient wisdom reflects the remarkable duality present in all substances around us. Every element, every molecule, every compound we encounter in life can either nourish us or harm us, depending on how, when, and how much we consume.

Even snake venom—a substance feared for its deadly potential—is, in its essence, a protein. Like any other protein, it can be broken down by the acids in our digestive system when ingested orally, rendering it harmless. Yes, theoretically, one can *drink* snake venom and survive without harm, as long as it does not enter the bloodstream.

The danger arises when that same venom enters the circulatory system directly—through a bite or an open wound. There, it mimics certain elements of our body, particularly iron, and competes for its binding sites. It interferes with the transport of oxygen by displacing iron in haemoglobin molecules. The body, though surrounded by oxygen, can no longer utilize it. And thus, the person dies not from lack of oxygen in the air, but from the inability to absorb and use it. This is called asphyxiation without suffocation—a cruel and quiet death, where life ebbs away despite the lungs being full.

Once in a dense forest near a quiet village lived a majestic King Cobra, proud and imposing, revered for its strength and feared for its deadly venom. It's very presence stirred fear—even the whisper of its movement would send shivers through spines. With enough venom to kill three or four grown humans, the snake wore its power like a crown. It slithered boldly through huts and granaries, hunting rodents and frogs, asserting its silent dominance over its domain.

The King Cobra had grown used to this fear—it fed not only on animals but on the trembling respect of men. It believed fear was power. Until one day, that illusion broke.

As the cobra returned to its nest, it encountered a group of ten young men—carefree students exploring the woods. To its surprise, they didn't flinch, didn't scream, didn't run. They stared at it casually, almost dismissively.

Stunned by the lack of fear, the King Cobra's pride was bruised. It couldn't accept this indifference. In a rush to prove its deadly worth, it struck—again and again—biting one after another in blind rage.

The first boy collapsed and died instantly. The second fell unconscious. The third fainted. But to the cobra's growing horror, the others—wounded but alive—grabbed sticks, stones, and courage, and beat the snake to death.

The mighty King Cobra, with all its venom and grandeur, died in a heap—not because it lacked power, but because it misjudged when to use it.

As Chanakya once said, *"**Even if a snake is not poisonous, it should pretend to be venomous.**"* This simple tale carries a profound truth: power, if used without wisdom, invites destruction.

In life, we often equate strength with dominance, and quick reaction with decisiveness. But uncontrolled reactions—like the cobra's—are not signs of power. They are signs of insecurity.

True strength lies in restraint. In knowing when to act and when to pause. In understanding that every action carries a consequence, and not every threat deserves a response.

We live in a world full of provocation—social, emotional, political. And we are wired to react: with anger, with fear, with ego. But reactions are reflexes; responses are reflections.

A reaction is like venom released blindly—it may prove your power, but it could cost you your life, your peace, or your relationships. A response is thoughtful, measured, and rooted in awareness. It protects without destroying, asserts without wounding.

In the end, the cobra died not because it lacked strength—but because it failed to understand the moment. May we all learn to be strong, not by striking, but by knowing "**When not to**."

"There are three sides for truth. Your side, my side and the right side—Magada"

Dog and the Four Puppies

In a forgotten corner of the world, a stray mother dog took shelter inside a discarded hume pipe—a hollow refuge amid the chaos of hunger and indifference. She had just given birth to four fragile puppies, tiny lives wrapped in the warmth of hope but born into the cruelty of scarcity. The mother, herself gaunt and weak, could not produce enough milk to nourish all her young. Their whimpers echoed through the pipe, cries not just of hunger, but of helplessness—a haunting symphony of survival.

The mother, torn between maternal instinct and the unyielding demands of the world, made a painful decision. She resolved to leave the pipe and search for food, though her heart trembled with the fear that her absence might invite danger. To protect her vulnerable children, she drew an invisible boundary at the mouth of the pipe—her own version of the mythical *Lakshman Rekha*—a line that symbolized safety, restraint, and obedience. With a heavy heart, she instructed her puppies not to cross it until her return. They promised. A silent pact was made between innocence and trust.

Time passed. The mother roamed the alleys, scouring the refuse of mankind, growing more feeble with every step. Fate was unkind. No morsel, no mercy. Meanwhile, back at the pipe, hunger clawed at the bellies of the puppies. Two of the elder ones, unable to bear the gnawing emptiness, broke their promise and crossed the sacred line. They scavenged the filth of the street—degrading themselves to survive. They quenched their thirst not with milk but with whatever the world had discarded, whatever their dignity could endure.

The younger two, despite their weaker bodies, clung to the promise. They stayed within the boundary, not out of strength, but out of conviction. They endured the slow torment of hunger, holding on to the sanctity of the word they had given.

When the mother returned, she was a shell of herself—starved, delirious, and defeated. She had found no food. Her instincts now warped by desperation, she did the unthinkable: she turned on her own, devouring the two obedient ones who had kept their vow. The sacred line had not saved them. Their honesty had not protected them. Their suffering had not been rewarded.

This tale, though brutal, whispers a solemn truth about life: goodness is not always shielded from tragedy. The world does not always favour the righteous, nor does it spare them from pain. Sometimes, those who walk the straight path are the first to fall. The straight trees, it is said, are the first to be cut in the forest.

Yet, the lesson here is not to condemn honesty, but to recognize its cost. Morality is a choice, not a guarantee. It is a path walked not for reward, but for meaning. And in a world where nature tests character without mercy, where outcomes often betray virtue, perhaps the ultimate nobility lies not in surviving—but in staying true to one's promise, even when no one is watching, even when the price is everything.

"Even thieves have their own laws—Magada"

Three Fugitives

In the underworld—in the silent alleys where justice is forgotten and morality walks with a limp—there exists a strange, unspoken order. A world run by men with blood on their hands, but oddly, boundaries in their hearts. The underworld.

People often imagine it as chaos, pure savagery, ruled by greed and gunpowder. But those who have danced long enough in the shadows know: even darkness has its code.

In this world, even killers pause when a line is drawn—not by law, but by legacy. Even when the price is high—when a contract is signed in whispers and paid in diamonds or debt—there are rules that even the most ruthless dare not violate.

One such principle is sacred: **No blood shall be spilled in front of the innocent.**

No matter how grave the crime, no matter how strong the hatred or how urgent the mission—**if the target is in the company of his children or his mother**, the gun stays holstered. The blade remains sheathed. The job waits.

The killer might follow him for hours... days... blending with crowds, watching from the shadows. But if the target holds a child's hand or walks beside a frail mother, the hunter becomes a ghost. He disappears without a trace, only to return when the man is alone—when his breath cannot traumatize the young, when death won't soak the white hair of a grieving mother in red.

It is not kindness. It is not guilt. It is principle—old, unshaken, and respected even by those who defy every other law.

This paradox of honour among killers may sound absurd to those who live within the comfort of law and order. But in the underworld, a man is only feared if his word means something—even if that word is delivered in silence, with a bullet.

Because in that world, reputation is currency. And a man who breaks the code may kill once, but he dies a thousand times in betrayal. No one trusts the man who shoots a father in front of his children. No one protects the butcher who stains motherhood with blood.

And so, they wait.

They wait with the patience of death itself—cold, calculating, quiet. They wait not out of mercy, but out of measure. Because even in the darkness, there are lines that must not be crossed.

We often think morality is reserved for saints and law-abiding citizens. But the truth is more complex. Even the most lawless of realms constructs its own ethics, born not from goodness, but from necessity. Why? Because without a code, even criminals would fall prey to chaos. And in chaos, no power lasts.

The underworld may live in shadows, but it survives through discipline. And its greatest secret is this: Even evil knows it cannot kill everything and still expect to rule.

There were three friends from the same region. They were all ambitious. They used to do robbery together. But when it comes to the share, they always used to fight. Though, they lived together, they never believed each other. There was a kingpin lived in the distant place. They all used to take his blessings before they do any robbery or dacoity.

There once were three companions who hailed from the same rugged region—men of sharp ambition and unrelenting desire. Bound by a common hunger for wealth and power, they formed a pact, engaging in thefts and raids across nearby towns. They moved together like shadows in the night, their hands united in crime but their hearts divided by suspicion.

Though they plotted and executed their acts together, the harmony ended the moment it was time to divide the spoils. Every success was followed by strife. Accusations flew over who deserved more, who took the greater risk, or who had been cleverer in the act. Their greed eclipsed any sense of brotherhood. They lived together in a fragile alliance, yet trust never made a home among them.

Despite their constant bickering, they remained loyal—if only outwardly—to a distant kingpin who resided far from their region. He was a silent patriarch of their ways, a figure they revered not out of love, but out of fear and necessity. Before each heist or act of banditry, they sought his symbolic blessings—perhaps to ward off guilt, or to lend legitimacy to their wrongdoing. He never intervened in their quarrels but was always the invisible string that held their chaotic unity.

Their world was marked not by peace, but by territorial obsession. They guarded their domain with the ferocity of wounded lions, allowing no outsiders to stake a claim. Competition was seen not as opportunity, but as threat. Their ambition stretched beyond their means, always eyeing a future drenched in control, luxury, and supremacy. Yet, beneath this dream lay a festering truth—they were enslaved by their own mistrust and consumed by their inability to coexist.

Their story was not one of unity, but of uneasy survival—a reminder that shared goals do not always foster loyalty, and ambition without character only multiplies enemies among friends.

The Final Journey

As fate would have it, one fine morning was destined to be their last together. The three men—bound not by brotherhood but by ambition and greed—had come to a dark convergence of thought. Each one, in the silent chambers of his own mind, had resolved to eliminate the other two and claim all their amassed wealth. They smiled at each other with the civility of wolves in sheep's skin, masking the venom that brewed within.

They planned a trip—a symbolic outing to mark their false unity. A vehicle was hired for the journey. But beneath the surface of this mundane arrangement, murder whispered in secret.

The first, restless and sleepless, waited until the others drifted into the comfort of slumber. At precisely 11:00 p.m., under the dim light of deceit, he crept to the vehicle and silently loosened the nuts on two wheels. A small twist of the spanner, a mechanical betrayal—his trap was set. The wheels would fail, he thought, and death would come dressed as an accident.

At 3:00 a.m., the second one awoke, unaware of the previous sabotage. In his own cloak of treachery, he approached the vehicle and removed a critical bolt from the brake system. Let them try to stop it, he smirked inwardly—the faster they drive, the surer their end.

The third, more patient, believed in poison over peril. As the sun's first pale rays reached the earth, he rose before the others and prepared a hearty breakfast. But it was no meal of goodwill. Each morsel was soaked in death. He laid it neatly on the dining table—warm, welcoming, and wicked.

Morning broke with deceptive calm. They dressed in silence, each hiding a death wish beneath their smiles. The two saboteurs, secretly intent on avoiding the ride they had doomed, lingered lazily, pretending to eat. The third, unaware of their hesitation, went to bathe, satisfied that his venom would do the work.

When he returned, water still dripping from his hair, he found a grotesque stillness in the room. His two comrades had collapsed mid-meal, twisted on their chairs, foam and vomit staining their lips. The poison had done its job too soon. The sight, though ghastly, gave him no pause. Guilt did not knock. Conscience did not stir. Survival had eclipsed all else.

He rushed. He packed the bags—bags heavy with wealth, blood, and betrayal. With trembling hands and a quickened breath, he ran to the vehicle—the very one now a death machine crafted by his own conspirators.

He turned the ignition. The engine roared like fate waking from sleep. The vehicle rolled. The road stretched forward—empty, silent, unforgiving.

Three men, united by greed, were undone not by their enemies, but by the mirror within. Each sought to outsmart the others. Each believed in their own invincibility. But in truth, they had all already died the moment they stopped trusting.

Trust is the invisible thread that weaves people together. When it breaks, no bond—be it of friendship, family, or fellowship—can hold. When greed replaces grace, even comrades become predators. And when betrayal becomes the norm, destruction follows—quietly, completely, inevitably.

In the theatre of life, some plots write themselves. And sometimes, the curtain falls not at the end—but in the middle of the act, when everyone forgets the script of humanity.

The Kingpin's Farewell

A few days later, the town wore a sombre veil. News of the three deaths—shocking yet shrouded in ambiguity—spread like wildfire. The streets buzzed with whispers, but no one spoke aloud what everyone silently suspected: betrayal from within.

Into this tense silence arrived the kingpin, the distant orchestrator of their brotherhood, their blessing-giver, and moral mirage. He came cloaked not in robes of power, but in the dignified fabric of grief. With great ceremony, he arranged a condolence meeting in the heart of the town. There were garlands, flickering candles, solemn words, and crafted sorrow. Photographs of the three men—now martyrs in the eyes of the public—stood framed upon the stage.

Standing before the gathering, the kingpin spoke with slow, measured emotion. "They were good men," he declared. "Brave, loyal friends... perhaps too bold for this world. Someone must have betrayed them. But their legacy will remain."

The crowd murmured, uncertain whether to believe or disbelieve. Truth, in such moments, becomes elastic—stretched between what is known, what is felt, and what must be accepted for peace to prevail.

The kingpin did not accuse. He did not explain. He simply took what was left behind—the wealth, the spoils of a thousand sins. There were no claimants, no heirs. Their possessions, tainted with blood and silence, passed into his hands not by right, but by power.

And then, quietly, he departed the town with the spoils, leaving behind echoes and ashes.

As the car rolled past the outskirts, where the noise of the town faded into barren dust, he pulled out his phone. Calmly, methodically, he began deleting messages—those cryptic exchanges he had sent to each of the three. Words that had once stirred fear, loyalty, or cunning—now wiped clean like chalk from a blackboard.

With a tap and a swipe, all digital fingerprints of his manipulation vanished.

Then, almost theatrically, he changed his display picture to a collage of the three deceased. Their smiling faces now fronted his public profile—a mourning gesture for the world to see. A digital tombstone, curated by the very hand that had fed their ambition, exploited their mistrust, and watched them destroy one another.

The kingpin's act was not merely one of self-preservation, but a portrait of how power insulates itself from consequence. In deleting the messages, he was not erasing evidence alone—he was erasing his moral obligation. Memory, in the modern age, lives on devices. And what can be deleted, can be denied.

His new display picture was more than a tribute; it was a masquerade. It allowed him to grieve without guilt, to mourn without involvement. It created a narrative: *"They were my loyal friends; I have lost them too."* When in truth, he had only lost pawns in a game he never truly played with his own hands.

There's a subtle irony here—those who kill with the mind rarely stain their fingers. They wear grief like a mask, they speak of loyalty over graves they helped dig. And society, craving closure more than truth, lets them.

This story isn't just about crime. It's a parable about how power, when devoid of conscience, can rewrite memory itself. The kingpin didn't escape justice—he transcended it, by owning the narrative.

"When life dumps on you, roll it like a dung beetle—Magada"

The Dung Beetle

I have always been fascinated by the dung beetle — a seemingly insignificant creature, yet carrying within it a profound lesson from nature. At first glance, it may appear as a lowly insect rolling waste across the ground. But pause and reflect, and you begin to see the wisdom embedded in its existence. The dung beetle does not complain, does not chase glory, nor seek validation. It simply does what it must — with purpose, consistency, and resilience. It transforms waste into life by laying its eggs inside what the world considers filth. In that, it reminds us that even what appears worthless can become a cradle of hope and new beginnings.

Nature, in its quiet brilliance, offers us countless teachers — if only we learn to observe. The dung beetle teaches us humility, focus, and perseverance. It reminds us that every being has its role, that dignity lies not in status but in purpose. In a world obsessed with image, the dung beetle calls us back to substance.

If we open our eyes and hearts, nature becomes a mirror — showing us what we need to unlearn, to evolve, and to live with deeper harmony. True wisdom is not in domination, but in alignment — in tuning ourselves to the rhythm of life around us. Only then we can live meaningfully, with reverence for all that lives and moves — even a beetle rolling its sacred burden beneath the stars.

In my journey through life, I have often come across people who seem to have failed — not because they made an attempt and didn't succeed, but because they never dared to try in the first place. It is a quiet kind of failure, one that is often masked by excuses, fear, or the comfort of the known. But in truth, I hesitate to even place them in the category of 'failure,' for to fail, one must have made an effort. One must have stepped into the arena, faced uncertainty, and risked loss.

There is dignity in failure that comes from genuine effort. The person who has failed after trying carries the weight of experience, the scars of courage, and a heart that was willing to strive. Such people are far more accomplished than those who never moved beyond contemplation. They are the ones who carry lessons, not regrets. Their 'failures' often become seeds of strength, resilience, and future success.

On the other hand, those who avoid trying—paralyzed by fear of judgement or defeat—remain untouched by both failure and growth. They are like seeds that refused to break open and missed the chance to become trees. Life doesn't honour mere intentions; it rewards action.

It recognizes the courage of those who stood up and said, 'Let me try,' even if the outcome was uncertain.

In the book of life, those who have failed with effort are written in ink; those who never tried are only faint shadows pencilled in the margins. True failure is not falling short—it is staying in the game till you win. It is choosing to compete, boldness over hesitation, and faith over doubt. And so, I say with certainty: those who failed after trying are far greater than those who never dared at all. The world remembers the players—the ones who stepped onto the field, who dared, who played—regardless of whether they won or lost. Ask yourself, do you recall the person who handed the World Cup trophy to Messi? Or the dignitary who presented the IPL trophy to the winning team in India? Likely not. Because history doesn't remember the presenters—it remembers the performers.

So stop waiting for perfect conditions or applause. Don't aim to be remembered for standing beside greatness—strive to be part of it. Step into your arena, embrace your calling, and play your game with all your heart. That's the only way to be remembered. Just that. Go, and play in your field

The Dung Beetle Within – A Story for Unemployed Youth

In the silent corners of the earth, far from admiration or spotlight, lives a tiny creature—the dung beetle. Just 10 milli meters in size, often dismissed as insignificant, this little insect performs one of nature's most astonishing feats. It can pull 1,411 times its own body weight—the human equivalent of lifting two fully loaded 18-wheel trucks.

Most would laugh at the idea of learning from a dung beetle. After all, it lives in waste, survives in struggle, and thrives in filth. But that is exactly where the lesson lies—for those who are walking through the muddy fields of unemployment, rejection, and hopelessness.

The Return of Reshi: A Journey from Drift to Determination

Reshi was once celebrated as a brilliant student—a boy who outshone many of his peers with his sharp mind and sky-high ambitions. Scoring an impressive 96.8 percentile in the Joint Entrance Examination, he secured admission to the Indian Institute of Information Technology (IIIT), Jabalpur, India, National Institute of Technology, Suratkal, Karnataka and finally leaving those two institutes, joined prestigious RV College of Engineering, Bangalore, a dream for many aspiring engineers across the country.

But life, as it often does, took a detour.

Somewhere along the way, Reshi was drawn into the fast-paced, glittering world of digital media. He became a successful influencer, earning not just popularity but a decent income. The thrill of instant validation and financial independence slowly eroded his interest in structured education. One decision followed another, and with the reluctant consent of his parents, he made a bold move—he discontinued his studies.

The world around him whispered in disappointment:

"Such a wasted potential..."
"A bright spark dimmed by distraction..."

But behind those whispers stood two silently hopeful figures—his parents. His father, an academician, and his mother, a postgraduate in Philosophy, were pained but patient. They understood that brilliance sometimes goes astray before it finds its true course.

And then came a moment. Not a grand epiphany or dramatic turning point—just a quiet, deep realization: Reshi began to believe again. Not because someone forced him to, but because something within him stirred—a voice that whispered louder than the world:

"You were meant for more."

With renewed purpose, he returned to college. Not as the same boy who left in confusion, but as a young man burning with resolve. He faced the impossible—14-18 subjects pending—and cleared them all in one determined stretch. The very subjects that once seemed like mountains were now stepping stones.

He had once convinced himself that he couldn't study, that academics were not for him. But one day of clarity, one decision of discipline, shattered that illusion. Today, Reshi is preparing for the Indian Administrative Service (IAS)—one of the toughest and most respected competitive exams in the world.

Whether he cracks it or not is beside the point. He is in the process with great positive energy…

What matters is that he reclaimed his journey. That he proved to himself—and to others—that failure is not the end, but a bend in the road, and that potential is never wasted as long as you're willing to pick it up again.

Sometimes, youth stumble not because they lack intelligence, but because they lose direction in a noisy world that rewards distraction. But those who turn inward, even briefly, often find a strength that can rebuild what was lost.

Reshi's story is not just about exams or engineering or IAS. It's about the courage to begin again. And that, more than marks or ranks, is the true test of greatness.

One evening, sitting on a dusty park bench, I watched an insect rolling a ball of dung across the path. Curious, I leaned closer. The beetle struggled, slipped, pushed again, and again—relentlessly. It didn't care about who watched or what filth it was rolling. It had a goal. It had a purpose.

This night, go and search: *"Strongest insect in the world"*. It will stun you:

"The dung beetle (*Anthophagus taurus*), 10 mm long, can pull 1,411 times its body weight—the human equivalent of lifting two fully loaded 18-wheelers."

You stare at the screen, then go and stand in front of the mirror. Say it yourself that "*If a beetle can drag mountains through dirt... why can't I pull myself through this phase?*"

That very night, you make decision to yourself: you wouldn't stop, no matter how dirty the path looked. you take up a pending work you wanted to finish. You learn new skills, you struggle, make mistakes, but never give up. Let the days turned to months. Opportunities come—not glamorous ones, but stepping stones. You grab every one of them.

Years later, you become leader by yourself and you will be addressing unemployed youths. In every motivational talk you start and end with the same line:

"If you feel worthless, jobless, or stuck, remember: the dung beetle doesn't complain about the dirt—it moves it. Find your strength. Pull your weight. You are stronger than you think."

Unemployment is not the end. It is the dirt you must walk through.
Society may mock your struggle, just as it mocks the dung beetle.
But strength is not in size or status—it is in how much you carry without giving up.

Be the dung beetle. Get inspired.
Lift... Roll... Move... Repeat.

"One day, your story will inspire someone who is sitting where you once sat—in silence, in doubt, in darkness. So start preparing now, for the time will come when you'll share that story with the world."

"In the food chain, every predator is also prey—Magada"

The Lion and Deer

Nature, in its infinite wisdom, has crafted every creature with a purpose—a role intricately woven into the grand design of life on Earth. From the tiniest insect to the largest mammal, each living being contributes to the balance and rhythm of the natural world.

Just because human beings, in their limited understanding, fail to recognize the value or function of a particular species does not mean it is without purpose. Our ignorance does not diminish its significance. A being's worth is not measured by our comprehension, but by its role in the ecological tapestry. When we label something as 'useless' or 'insignificant,' we expose more about the limits of our perception than about the creature itself. In truth, nature wastes nothing. Everything exists for a reason—even if that reason lies beyond our current grasp.

To live in harmony with nature is to acknowledge that every life form matters, and that humility is the first step toward wisdom. Let us not judge the value of life by our convenience, but by the deeper truth that everything has its rightful place in the universe.

When we walk through a forest or a wildlife sanctuary, it's not uncommon to spot large herds of deer grazing peacefully. Their numbers have been rising steadily, thanks to growing public awareness about wildlife conservation and the strict enforcement of the Wildlife Protection Act. However, there's another, often overlooked, reason behind this surge in their population—the sharp decline in their natural predators.

In the past, the ecological balance was maintained through the presence of apex predators such as tigers, lions, and leopards, which kept the population of herbivores like deer in check. But over the years, due to habitat loss, poaching, and human interference, the population of these big cats has dwindled drastically.

Interestingly, even though predators like tigers or leopards may give birth to 4–5 cubs, and deer typically produce only 1–2 calves, the population dynamics still favour the prey. This is because without sufficient predators to control them, deer and similar species thrive and multiply rapidly, leading to a prey-heavy ecosystem.

This shift is a reminder of how interconnected and delicate our natural systems are. The disappearance of predators doesn't just affect one species—it ripples across the food chain, altering the balance that nature so carefully maintains. Conservation, therefore, isn't just about protecting individual animals; it's about preserving the entire symphony of life in its intended harmony.

In the wild, when a predator such as a tiger or lion becomes hungry, it instinctively turns toward a herd of deer or similar prey. This primal chase is not random—it is a finely tuned act within nature's grand design. Most animals, like deer or fish, tend to live in groups. This isn't accidental. Group living enhances their chances of survival, improves their foraging efficiency, and provides safety through collective vigilance.

However, when danger strikes—when the predator launches its chase—the entire group scatters and runs. It is in that moment of chaos that nature conducts one of its oldest and most merciless tests: a trial of speed, strength, and endurance. The fittest individuals surge ahead, while the weaker ones struggle to keep pace. Eventually, it is the slowest, the weakest that get caught.

This seemingly cruel process is actually nature's way of refining its population—a natural method of culling the vulnerable to ensure that only the resilient survive and reproduce. It strengthens the genetic pool, maintaining the overall vitality of the species.

Such predator-prey dynamics are not just about survival. They are about balance, selection, and evolution. Nature does not reward sympathy; it rewards suitability. In this system, even death has a purpose—it nurtures the life that remains.

This concept extends beyond the forest and applies metaphorically to human society as well. In competitive environments—whether in business, education, or personal growth—those who are stronger, better prepared, or more adaptable often surge ahead. While empathy and compassion are human values that we cherish, nature teaches us a deeper truth: strength must be 'cultivated,' not assumed. And sometimes, falling behind is not just a personal loss, but part of a larger process of natural order.

In any given situation—be it life, career, relationships, or competition—one fundamental principle prevails: you must strive to be better in your chosen field. Excellence is not just a virtue; it is a necessity for survival and relevance. From the simplest life forms like fungi to the most evolved beings like humans, nature has always favoured the most adaptable, resilient, and efficient. This is the essence of natural selection. The tree that stretches higher gets the sunlight. The bird that flies stronger survives the storm. The mind that thinks sharper finds the path forward.

Nature is impartial—it does not reward the mediocre; it supports the best-equipped to thrive. Hence, every living being, every gene, is locked in an eternal quest to prove its worth—to evolve, to adapt, and to rise above the average.

This journey isn't about guaranteed success. You may stumble. You may lose. You may fail. But the deeper truth lies not in the result but in your willingness to be part of the process. The fish that swims upstream may not reach the spawning ground, but its effort defines its purpose. Similarly, you must remain in the flow of growth, constantly refining yourself—not for applause, but for survival and fulfilment.

To withdraw is to decay. To stop trying is to invite irrelevance. In a world that is constantly changing, only those who keep evolving stay alive in spirit, not just in body. So wherever you are, whoever you are—be better. Learn deeper. Work harder. Dream stronger. It's not about being the best in the world; it's about being the best version of yourself in the field you've chosen. That alone is your tribute to nature and your testament to life.

"Genes never cheat—Magada"

The Selfish Gene

Genes are too selfish. They produce their own copies and go on replicating them. No cheating in genes. They all want their copies to survive. Have anytime wonder why these honey bees work for each other defeating the law of competition in the nature.

At the very core of life, beneath the surface of flesh and thought, lies a hidden driver—the gene. Cold, precise, and ancient, genes carry the blueprint of life itself. Yet, they are not benevolent architects. On the contrary, genes are selfish. Their ultimate goal is singular and unwavering: to survive by replicating themselves, generation after generation.

Every living being—be it a worm in the soil, a lion in the wild, or a human with dreams—is simply a vehicle for genes to propagate. There is no room for generosity in this microscopic empire. Each gene competes, silently but relentlessly, to ensure its version of the truth—its code—is passed on.

And yet, nature throws at us an astonishing paradox: the honeybee.

Have you ever stood near a beehive? Observed how hundreds of bees work tirelessly—not for themselves, but for each other? They gather nectar, build intricate combs, defend their hive fiercely, and even sacrifice their lives when threatened. Here, the law of the jungle seems reversed. There is no visible selfishness, no one bee hoarding honey, no obvious survival of the fittest. So what is really happening?

The answer lies deeper in the elegant dance between selfish genes and collective behaviour.

The worker bee, which stings and dies to protect the hive, is not acting out of emotion or ethics. It's acting under a genetic strategy known as kin selection. Even though the worker bee may not reproduce, its genes are still present in the queen and in the thousands of sisters in the colony. By protecting the hive, the worker is indirectly ensuring the survival of its own genetic material. What appears to be selfless is actually a higher-order selfishness—not of the individual, but of the gene.

This is nature's irony: cooperation is often the most successful form of competition. Bees don't betray each other, not because they are saints, but because their evolutionary design makes betrayal counterproductive. Their collective survival ensures the continuity of their shared genetic legacy.

So next time you see a bee at work, remember—beneath its wings hums a timeless principle: The gene is selfish. But sometimes, the smartest way to survive is through selfless behaviour.

This story of bees tells us something about ourselves, too. As humans, we are not entirely different. While we are driven by our own instincts to succeed, we flourish most when we collaborate, when we protect the greater good, when we act not just for self, but for something larger.

Because in the end, the gene may be selfish—but the story of life is built on interdependence.

Why Do Honeybee Workers Support Each Other Without Competing?

At first glance, honeybee society seems to defy Darwinian logic. In a world supposedly ruled by "survival of the fittest," why would worker bees — who do not reproduce — support each other selflessly, serve a single queen, and even sacrifice their lives for the hive?

The answer lies in a deeper and more nuanced concept of evolution called kin selection and inclusive fitness.

1. **Kin Selection**: Genes Over Individuals

In honeybees (as well as ants and wasps), workers are highly related to each other due to a genetic system called haplodiploidy:

- Females (workers and queens) are diploid (have two sets of chromosomes),
- Males (drones) are haploid (have one set, coming only from the queen).

This means that sister worker bees share about 75% of their genes, which is more than they would share with their own offspring (only 50%).

So, from a gene's point of view, helping a sister survive and reproduce is more beneficial than reproducing oneself.

This is kin selection — a strategy where individuals act altruistically toward close relatives, because by helping them survive and reproduce, they are still promoting their own genes indirectly.

2. **Inclusive Fitness**: Beyond Individual Success

Inclusive fitness expands the idea of evolutionary success. It says that an organism's success is not just about how many offspring it produces, but also about how many related individuals' offspring survive due to its help.

So, when worker bees:

- Feed larvae,
- Defend the hive,
- Build and clean combs,
- Sacrifice themselves in defense...

...they are all actions that increase the survival of the queen (who produces all the eggs) and their sisters — which means their shared genes are still being passed on.

3. **No Reproductive Competition Among Workers**

The queen bee produces chemical signals (pheromones) that suppress the reproductive abilities of the workers. Even if a worker wanted to lay eggs, her biology and the social order prevent it. This reduces internal competition and channels all energy into the survival of the hive, which is essentially a superorganism — a collective body made up of thousands of individuals functioning as one.

4. **Evolutionary Stability of Cooperation**

In honeybee evolution, cooperation turned out to be more efficient than competition. The entire colony thrives better when there is:

- Division of labour,
- Shared purpose,
- No infighting.

This cooperation allows the colony to survive threats, store resources, regulate temperature, and raise new queens. It's natural selection at the level of the group and the gene, not necessarily the individual.

Honeybee workers support each other without competing because:

- They are highly genetically related (especially sisters),

- Their inclusive fitness is maximized by helping the queen and each other,
- Reproductive roles are biologically restricted, reducing rivalry,
- The colony as a whole is the unit of evolutionary success — not the individual.

Among honeybee workers, the percentage of shared genes is approximately 75% — but this is only true under specific conditions due to their unique genetic system called haplodiploidy.

Why 75%?

Honeybees follow a haplodiploid sex-determination system:

- Queen (female) is diploid (2 sets of chromosomes).
- Drone (male) is haploid (1 set, from the queen only — no father).

How Sister Workers Get 75% Relatedness:

- The queen mates with a single drone (monandry).
- Drones produce sperm that are all genetically identical.
- When the queen lays fertilized eggs (future workers), each gets:
    - 50% of the queen's genes, randomly selected.
    - 100% identical genes from the drone.

On average, the coefficient of relatedness between full sisters (worker bees from the same queen and same drone) becomes:

- **0.5 (from the queen) × 0.5 (chance of sharing) = 0.25**
- **0.5 (from the drone) × 1.0 (identical) = 0.5**
  → 0.25 + 0.5 = 0.75 **or** 75% shared genes

Important Caveat: In nature, queens often mate with multiple drones (polyandry), reducing the average relatedness among workers to around 25% to 75%, depending on mating frequency.

Why It Matters: This high relatedness (75%) among full sisters is why kin selection evolved in honeybee societies — workers don't reproduce, but help raise their sisters, which passes on more of their own genes than having offspring themselves.

The essence of what I'm attempting to convey lies in the deeper philosophy of survival — not merely of the individual, but of the lineage, the legacy, the very thread of life that has wound its way through generations to arrive at you. You are not a random occurrence in nature; you are the result of countless survival strategies executed with instinct, intelligence, adaptation, and sacrifice of your forefathers. Each of your ancestors, knowingly or unknowingly, contributed to preserving a genetic line that was strong enough, resilient enough, and adaptable enough to overcome time, disease, war, famine, and circumstance.

This genetic line — your life — is not ordinary. It is the victorious residue of a million forgotten battles. You carry within you the best that your family tree could preserve and pass on. It is your duty, not in a rigid biological sense, but in a conscious, moral, and philosophical sense, to preserve that lineage with dignity and wisdom.

This doesn't simply mean reproducing. It means selecting an opposite — a life partner — with discernment and responsibility. One who complements your strengths, elevates your weaknesses, and contributes to the environment in which the next link in the chain — your children, your legacy — will grow. It is in this thoughtful union, in this purposeful selection, that the quality of the gene pool is refined, not just in terms of biology, but in ethics, emotions, intellect, and culture.

You are not merely passing down genes; you are passing down a possibility — the possibility of a better human. You are the bridge between your ancestors and the unborn. So live consciously. Choose wisely. And remember, evolution has brought you here, but your choices will determine who comes after you.

"Earth was not made for humans alone. Every creature has the same right to live here —Magada"

Jelly Fish

While interacting with coastal communities, I often noticed fishermen hauling their nets only to find them tangled with hundreds of jellyfish. Most of these jellyfish, perceived as a nuisance, were tossed back into the sea or discarded carelessly upon reaching the landing centres. For a long time, even I regarded them as one of the 'waste' organisms of the ocean—unwanted, unimportant, and devoid of utility.

Yet, amidst this seemingly casual disregard, a thought would stir within me: ***Why would nature—or if you believe, a divine force—create a being with no purpose?*** Can anything that survives the rigorous filters of evolution truly be meaningless?

It struck me then that our perception of value is often shaped by utility to humans. If something cannot be consumed, sold, or easily understood, we brand it as 'useless'. But is that not a narrow lens to view the marvels of nature?

The jellyfish, for all its delicate beauty and ghostlike form, plays intricate roles in the marine ecosystem—regulating plankton populations, serving as food for certain turtles and fish, and participating in complex biogeochemical cycles. Its role may not directly touch our dinner plates or market stalls, but its presence is not accidental.

Just because we do not fully understand its contribution—or worse, just because it inconveniences us—how can we hastily label it as waste? Nature doesn't operate on human terms. Everything created and sustained in this web of life has a role, whether we see it or not.

This realization brings with it a profound sense of humility. It reminds us that just because we do not understand something does not mean it lacks significance. Ignorance is never a measure of worth. Simply because a life form offers no apparent utility to human needs, it doesn't imply it has no rightful purpose or place in the grand design of existence.

Before we delve deeper into understanding the jellyfish—an organism so often dismissed—I would like to make a bold and necessary declaration: ***This Earth was not crafted solely for human beings.*** Humanity, or ***Homo sapiens,*** is merely one species among an estimated 8.7 million known life forms that inhabit this planet.

To assume that we are the centre of creation is a fallacy rooted in ego, not in science or wisdom. We share this planet with countless other beings—each playing a role in the balance of ecosystems that have evolved over billions of years. The web of life is intricate and interconnected, and every creature, no matter how obscure or misunderstood, contributes to its strength and sustainability.

The jellyfish may drift silently through the ocean currents, but its presence whispers to us an essential truth: purpose is not always visible, and significance is not always measured by human standards. To live wisely on this Earth, we must learn to see beyond ourselves—to respect life in all its forms, not just those that serve us directly

The jellyfish is considered the largest known planktonic organism in the world. Despite possessing soft, flowing tentacles and a bell-shaped body that allows for gentle pulsating movement, it lacks the ability to swim against ocean currents. This inability to control its path in water defines its place among plankton — organisms that drift with the movement of water rather than navigate it actively.

Its grace and rhythm in the ocean may appear intentional, even poetic, but in truth, the jellyfish surrenders to the direction of the tide. It is a reminder that not all creatures who float do so by choice — some are designed to move with the flow, not against it.

This categorization is not about size or structure, but about control — or rather, the lack of it. Plankton, by definition, are at the mercy of the water's whims, and the jellyfish, despite its size and appearance, is no exception. It teaches us that in nature, appearance is never the whole story. Strength and purpose do not always equate to control. Sometimes, even the most captivating beings must learn the art of drifting — not out of weakness, but as part of a grand design.

Jellyfish, though seemingly delicate and transparent, employ several camouflaging strategies that help them survive in the ocean — both as predators and as prey. Their survival depends largely on their ability to blend into their environment, and here's how they do it:

Transparency – The Ultimate Cloak

Most jellyfish are nearly 95% water, making them almost invisible in their watery habitat. Their translucent or transparent bodies allow light to pass through, making it extremely hard for predators (or prey) to detect them. From the philosophical note, *Sometimes, survival is about not being seen, not because you're weak — but because you're wise.* They are Bioluminescence in nature which distract and dazzle the predator. Some jellyfish can produce light using bioluminescent cells, which can serve as:

- A startle display to confuse predators.

- A decoy light to redirect attacks away from vital organs.
- A way to attract prey in the deep sea.
- Example: The *Atolla jellyfish* produces a flashing light when disturbed — like a burglar alarm to summon bigger predators that may scare off the threat.

Reflective Surfaces – Mirror Camouflage

Some jellyfish have iridescent or reflective tissues that reflect the surrounding colours of the ocean. This helps them mirror their environment, especially under shifting light in shallow waters.

- Counter-illumination camouflage – reflecting ambient light to blend with the background.
- Effect: Helps avoid predators approaching from below or above.

Minimal Shadow Casting

Thanks to their gelatinous and almost see-through body structure, jellyfish cast very little shadow, even when exposed to sunlight from above.

- Advantage: Less likely to be noticed by predators below — especially in the sunlit epipelagic zone (surface waters).

Shape and Movement

Their fluid, undulating motion mimics the gentle movement of ocean currents. This natural drifting helps them look like passive parts of the environment (e.g., floating debris or part of a plankton cloud).

Jellyfish, often misunderstood and underestimated, play a vital role in the marine food web. They are a primary source of nourishment for sea turtles, and together, both species serve as living indicators of a healthy, balanced ocean ecosystem. When their populations begin to decline, it's more than just a biological concern—it signals a deeper unravelling of ecological harmony.

Interestingly, the concept doesn't end with nature. Even in human societies, we encounter individuals who may seem out of place or difficult to understand—our own kind of 'jellyfish.' They may not fit into conventional roles or expectations, but that doesn't mean they're dispensable. Just as in nature, every presence has its place. Rather than attempting to eliminate such individuals or avoid them entirely, we must learn to coexist—sometimes with caution, but always with awareness.

Many beachgoers, driven by curiosity or ignorance, have touched jellyfish—intentionally or by accident—only to find their skin irritated with rashes. What we perceive as a nuisance is, in fact, the jellyfish's natural defense. It does not bite or chase; it simply defends itself with what nature has equipped it.

We humans wear clothes to protect our bodies; jellyfish use their stinging cells to protect theirs. It's not aggression, but survival. In the same way, when people act out or seem abrasive, sometimes it's not hostility but a defense born of their own life experiences. Understanding this can change how we see both the ocean's creatures and each other.

Lessons from the Jellyfish: A Reflection on Survival, Struggle, and the Strength of Simplicity

Even the most fragile and directionless creatures in the ocean—like jellyfish—manage to survive and thrive in the vast, competitive, and unpredictable waters of the sea. They drift with the currents, yet they are not helpless. They adapt through camouflage, they defend themselves when threatened, and they persist despite their vulnerability. They neither chase power nor dominate others, yet they endure in an environment full of predators and uncertainty.

This quiet resilience of jellyfish stands as a powerful metaphor for human life. In contrast, human beings—who live in organized societies, with intelligence, shelter, communication, and choices—often falter emotionally when confronted with life's challenges. Some are driven to hopelessness by seemingly trivial troubles, forgetting that survival is not about winning over others, but about flowing with life, adapting, and supporting one another.

If jellyfish, without a brain or spine, can navigate the trials of nature and sustain themselves with grace, then surely, we—gifted with awareness and the ability to love, think, and build—can find the strength to rise above our fears, insecurities, and ego-driven conflicts.

Let us learn from the smallest of life forms that survival doesn't demand superiority—it asks for resilience, harmony, and humility. No life is insignificant; every creature is a part of a larger system. Cooperation, not competition, is nature's true law. When we embrace this truth, we no longer measure life by success or failure—but by the compassion we carry and the courage to keep going and that's the life.

“Physics might have been simpler if the apple tree had fallen on Newton—Magada”

Escaping the Gravity

In the vast expanse of society, whenever an individual dares to do something new — to rise above the mundane and touch the edges of creativity or transformation — they are seldom met with open arms. The world, more often than not, greets such boldness with doubt, ridicule, and subtle resistance. Why?

Because every society has an invisible gravitational pull. This pull does not want change; it wants comfort. It seeks sameness. It desires predictability. When you rise, you disturb this predictable rhythm. Your ascent becomes a mirror in which others are forced to confront their own stillness, their own hesitations, and their abandoned dreams.

They say things like:

- "This won’t work."
- "Don’t be foolish."
- "Who do you think you are?"

But these aren't statements about your path — they are projections of their own fear of flight. They are the echoes of their own grounded existence. And when enough such voices rise around you, they can become a whirlpool of disbelief, sucking you into a cycle of self-doubt and mediocrity. Some lose themselves forever in this spiral.

But you must learn to escape the gravity.

Not by fighting it aggressively. Not by trying to prove anything. But by rising silently — like a hot air balloon that simply becomes too light to be held back. Your first leap into the space of the uncommon must be inward. You must lighten yourself of the need for approval, of the fear of isolation, of the burden of being understood by all.

The moment you do this, something magical happens: You rise to a space beyond the gravity of the common, where your vision, not their verdict, defines your direction.

And yet, detachment is not always easy. Old friends, familiar circles, even cherished companions may not understand the journey you embark on. You may not be able to sever ties openly — nor must you always do so. Sometimes, the wiser path is not to leave them, but to evolve within their presence. Be there, but be unmoved. Laugh with them, but think deeper. Share space, but not your soul's compass.

In a world that wants you to blend in, your greatest act of courage is to remain uniquely yourself. Rise not with rebellion, but with stillness. Let your silence become the sound of elevation.

As stars are born out of collapsing chaos, you too must allow your discomfort, your separation, and your doubt to birth something higher — a self that no longer needs to be pulled, but one that can guide.

The Story of the Deaf Frog

You may have heard this many times before — perhaps so often that it seems familiar. Yet, I invite you to read it once more. Why? Because the right stories, when revisited, act as reminders that anchor us to our purpose. In a world full of distractions and doubts, we must continuously nourish our thoughts with the right messages to maintain our momentum and stay on a positive path. Repetition is not redundancy; it is reinforcement.

Once upon a time, a group of frogs decided to organize a climbing competition. The goal was to reach the top of a tall tower.

A huge crowd gathered to watch the event and cheer for the contestants. As the race began, no one in the crowd actually believed that the frogs could reach the top.

You could hear voices like:

- "Oh, it's too difficult!"
- "They'll never make it."
- "The tower is too high!"

As the frogs struggled upward, one by one began falling back — discouraged by what they heard.

But one little frog kept climbing steadily.

The crowd continued shouting:

- "It's impossible!"
- "Give up!"

Still, that one frog didn't stop. He climbed and climbed… and finally reached the top!

Everyone was stunned. When the other frogs and reporters asked him how he managed to do it, they discovered something amazing:

The little frog was deaf.

Sometimes, the best way to succeed is to ignore the noise and discouragement around you.

Stay focused on your goal, believe in your ability, and don't let negativity pull you down. Be like the deaf frog — climb with courage, not with approval.

"Truth walks, while falsehood runs—Magada"

Righteousness Beyond Recognition

It was 10:30 p.m. when we reached the bus stop in Mangalore. The air was still, the night quiet — except for the scattered footsteps of people trying to catch the final bus of the day. That last bus, number 44C, ran from *State Bank Bus Station* to *Someshwar Beach*, passing through our college near Ekkur. We—myself, Sathish, and Shivaram—after our working drinks in some hotel, ran to the bus stop, hurried to the front entrance of the bus, which was just about to depart.

Shivaram boarded first, but just as Sathish and I were stepping in, a young woman in a burkha rushed forward. She wore high-heeled sandals and, as she tried to step in, she slipped. Instinctively, Sathish reached out from inside the bus and held her hand, and I supported her from behind to prevent a fall. We helped her regain balance and assisted her onto the bus. She quietly moved to the front row and took her seat.

A few moments later, a well-built man, presumably her husband, climbed aboard and began shouting at us. His tone was harsh, filled with anger and suspicion. He accused us of inappropriate behaviour for having touched his wife. We tried to explain — gently, respectfully — that we had only helped her. There was no indecency in our action, only concern and instinctive human empathy.

But our words were bounced back by a wall of distrust. The man wasn't listening. He was blinded by emotion, ego, perhaps even cultural sensitivity — and to him, our truth didn't matter. He further criticized us for boarding from the "ladies' entrance," which we did only because it was the last bus and there was urgency in the moment. We were young, and Mangalore's nights didn't offer too many options past 10:45.

I looked toward the woman we had helped — the only person who truly knew what had happened. A single word from her could have dissolved the misunderstanding. But she didn't turn toward us. Not a glance, not a nod — just silence.

With shame and helplessness, we walked to the back of the bus and took our seats. That night, guilt kept me awake. Not because we had done wrong, but because we were not able to prove that we were right. And the one person who could have spoken the truth remained silent.

The Paradox of Goodness

In that moment, I was introduced to a painful truth — doing the right thing does not always reward you with recognition or even protection. Sometimes, doing good will hurt you. Sometimes, it will bring suspicion, insult, and injustice. And the worst part? The world often lacks the patience or empathy to investigate goodness.

Should we then stop helping? Should we, from that experience, decide never again to help another woman, especially someone from a community we assume might not accept our help? Should we let misunderstanding breed prejudice in us?

No. That would be a betrayal of our own soul.

To let one misjudgement redefine our nature is to let darkness win. The world needs fewer people who react and more people who remain steady in goodness, even when unacknowledged.

Righteousness is not Measured by Applause

We must live by an inner compass — one that is not swayed by the applause of the crowd or the fear of judgment. That night, though we were humiliated, I chose to continue being who I was — someone who helps when help is needed, regardless of how the act is interpreted.

True character is revealed not when we are rewarded for being right, but when we continue being right even after being punished for it.

This experience reminded me that silence is not always betrayal, and misunderstanding is not always malice. People carry their own fears and limits. They act not always based on reason, but on wounds unseen. But we, as individuals, must not let their blindness dull our light.

Do what is right — not for reward, not for recognition — but because that is who you are.

"We must mature with our damage," because the moment you compromise your values to match the world's fears, you lose the only thing that truly matters: your integrity.

"Matriphagy (Babies eating their own mother)— nature's ultimate testament to a mother's sacrifice. — Magada"

The Spider

In the quiet corner of an old, forgotten library, a small spider began its work.

No spotlight fell on it. No applause echoed. No one paused to admire. And yet, thread by thread, the creature moved with intent, weaving its masterpiece of engineering and elegance.

Its web — a symphony of symmetry — was a marvel far beyond what most humans could ever create with machines or mathematics. It required no measurement tools, no blueprints, no reassurances. Just the wisdom woven into its instinct, passed silently through generations of unnoticed existence.

People are often mesmerized by the fantasy of *Spiderman* — the hero who swings across skyscrapers and defies gravity. But rarely do they pause to honour the real spider, whose daily act of survival holds deeper lessons than any fiction ever could.

The Sacred Thread of Purpose

Unlike creatures that hoard or conquer, the spider does not chase more than it needs. It builds not to dominate, but to survive — and it does so with beauty.

Each web is a monument to its clarity of purpose. It doesn't boast. It doesn't compare. It doesn't wait for applause. It simply does what it was born to do, again and again — even when the wind tears it down, or a careless hand brushes it away.

The spider teaches us: when your work is an expression of your being, destruction is not the end — it's just a signal to begin again.

The Dance of Stillness

Unlike the restless energy that defines much of human life, the spider knows the value of stillness. It doesn't rush. It waits. It sits — not in laziness, but in silent readiness.

How many of us can sit still and trust our creation to bring the reward? How many of us can build without needing validation?

In the spider's quiet wait lies a profound lesson in patience — that not all effort looks like movement, and not all movement leads to meaning.

Symmetry Amidst Chaos

The world is chaotic. Winds shift. People disappoint. Structures crumble. But look at a spider's web — delicate, yes, but also fiercely resilient. Even in the most uncertain corners of the world — between broken walls, swaying grass, or forgotten furniture — the spider builds something that holds form in the formless.

In chaos, find your centre. In destruction, begin again. In stillness, be prepared. These are the silent mantras of the spider.

You Are the Weaver

What if we all lived like spiders? Not in fear, but in craftsmanship. Not in comparison, but in commitment. Not to impress, but to express.

Like the spider, your greatest strength lies not in your appearance or noise, but in the quiet work you do when no one is watching. Your ideas, your struggles, your growth — they are the strands of your own web. They may be invisible to others now, but one day, they will catch the light.

In the end, the spider does not complain about the breeze that broke its web. It does not curse the hand that swept away its creation. It simply climbs back, and builds again — better, stronger, quieter.

So must we.

Because greatness is not built in noise. It is spun, thread by thread, in resilience, clarity, and purpose — just like the spider does, in the forgotten corners of the world, one silent masterpiece at a time.

The Mother's Sacrifice

In the quiet corners of nature, the spider weaves more than silk—it weaves the very fabric of sacrifice and survival. Most spiders lay between 20 to 300 eggs at once, each one a fragile vessel of potential life. These eggs are carefully wrapped in silken sacs, hidden beneath leaves, nestled in crevices, or suspended in the delicate threads of a web—places where life begins in silence and secrecy. Within one to four weeks, the eggs hatch, and the cycle of life unfurls.

Yet in some extraordinary species, like *Stegodyphus*—a social spider—the bond between mother and offspring transcends instinct and enters the realm of profound devotion. Here, the mother does not simply protect her young; she offers her very being as sustenance. In a biological act akin to mythic sacrifice, the mother allows her spiderlings to consume her body, giving them life through her death. This phenomenon, known as **matriphagy**, is not just a behavioural trait—it is a lesson in the ultimate selflessness, where love is written not in emotion but in action.

In other cases, such as with jumping spiders, the maternal gesture takes a gentler form—regurgitating pre-digested food for the spiderlings. It is a tender moment in the otherwise unsentimental wilderness—a whisper of nurturing care amidst the web of predation.

Thus, the spider teaches us that even in the smallest of beings, the forces of care, sacrifice, and continuation of life echo with a quiet dignity. Nature, through the spider, reveals a deeper truth: that parenthood, in its most primal form, is not a role—it is a surrender.

"Brain drain is not a misnomer; it truly happens when you disconnect from your roots —Magada"

The Last Salute She Never Saw

Devinder Sigh once commanded battalions, braved borders, and walked fearlessly through battlefields soaked in smoke and silence. A retired military officer—stoic, disciplined, and full of quiet pride—he had lived most of his life in uniform, guarding the nation while his wife guarded the home.

She was the quiet general of the domestic front. While he chased orders and medals, she chased school fees, groceries, and the warmth of a humble kitchen. They were a unit—two soldiers in different wars. She never asked for more than his presence in the evenings and his hand during festivals. And even that, she learned to live without.

They were blessed with two sons—Prabjith and Debjith—both raised with firm discipline and quiet pride. Growing up in the structured environment of military schools, the boys imbibed values of order, hard work, and respect. They excelled in academics, earning top ranks and eventually gaining admission to the prestigious Indian Institutes of Technology (IITs)—a dream that many aspire to but few achieve.

Their brilliance didn't stop at the borders of India. After completing their education, Prabjith secured a high-paying job in the United States, while Debjith built a successful career in Germany. For the parents, it was a moment of immense pride—like many families from Haryana, they saw their sons' migration to the West not as a separation, but as a symbol of success. It was the modern dream—the ultimate proof that their sacrifices had borne fruit.

The sons married in grand ceremonies, filled with music, rituals, and hundreds of guests. The weddings were nothing short of regal, orchestrated with all the joy and dignity that the parents could muster. And then, life moved on. The newlyweds returned to their adopted countries and settled into comfortable lives—busy, ambitious, and far away.

Communication became occasional. A few calls now and then—on festivals, birthdays, or during moments of obligation. Yet, the parents never complained. They didn't expect gifts or grand gestures. They didn't demand frequent visits or emotional theatrics. Their love was simple, patient, and quiet—grateful even for those brief calls that arrived across oceans and time zones.

They asked for little, and received even less—but never measured love in frequency. After all, as parents, they had given everything without keeping a ledger.

When retirement came, he thought he would finally give her the time she never asked for but always deserved. But age had other plans. Illness crept in like an uninvited guest, and one morning, without ceremony or fanfare, she exhaled her last breath.

He sat beside her lifeless body, not as a soldier now, but as a husband stripped of rank, helpless and alone. Calls were made. His children—well-settled abroad and in other cities—responded with silence, excuses, or indifference. "Flight is too expensive." "Too short notice." "Boss won't allow leave." "We'll come next month to see you, pappa."

Next month.

She was wrapped in white cloth that evening. No sons or daughters to carry her. No last glance. No forehead kiss. Only neighbours, a few old colleagues, and the priest. He stood by her pyre, back straight, eyes steady—like he did before every operation. But inside, his heart shattered like a landmine had gone off within.

As the flames rose, he whispered—not in anger, but in an aching calm—
"You stood by them when they learned to walk... and now they couldn't take a step toward you one last time."

He lit the fire. It was not just a body that burned—it was a lifetime of silent sacrifices, forgotten phone calls, unopened letters, and unspoken gratitude.

Not all abandonment is loud. Sometimes, it's just absence—cold, casual, and cruel. The soldier who once saluted the flag with pride now gave his final salute to the woman who bore everything in silence. And her children missed the only war she ever lost.

"Light travels faster than sound; that's why some people look brighter before they speak — Magada"

The Light House

The instant sight returns to the blind, the stick — once an extension of their very being — is abandoned, forgotten like an old shadow. When the clouds retreat and the last drop of rain slips away, the umbrella, once a sheltering sky, becomes an awkward burden in the hand. When dawn spills over the hills and night's curtain lifts, the torch that carved light out of darkness lies cold and useless. Such is the rhythm of our hearts — treasures in the storm, trinkets in the calm — until fate circles back, and we once again grope for the very things we had cast aside.

When you are far out in the deep ocean, there is no sign of land, no silhouette of a lighthouse to guide you. The waves stretch endlessly in every direction, and all you have is the steady hum of the wind and the pulse of your own heartbeat. At such a distance, even the tallest lighthouse is invisible — but that does not mean it isn't there. You must keep moving until you reach that point where the naked eye can finally catch its faint glimmer.

Life works the same way. When you have a strong purpose, you may not see the end goal at first, but something inside you — that unshakable *gut feeling* — acts like a compass, quietly urging you onward. It doesn't shout; it simply points, unwavering, in the direction you must go. Along the way, hope becomes your wind, love your anchor, dreams your sails, and passion the current beneath you, carrying you through the rough waters.

In the sea, speed means little if your course is wrong — a fast ship heading the wrong way only takes you further from safety. Likewise, in life, it's not how quickly you move, but whether you are moving in the right direction. The ocean teaches us this truth gently but firmly: find your compass, trust it, and keep moving. Eventually, the light will appear — not because it suddenly came into existence, but because you finally reached the point where you could see it.

There is great poem written by Dr K S Narasimha Swamy that goes like this, "Deepavu Ninnade..GaaLiyu Ninnade... Aaradirali... BeLakoo.. KaDaloo Ninnade...HaDagoo Ninnade, MuLugadirali Badukoo...." Which rough translates to **"The lamp is yours... the wind is yours... let the light never fade... the ocean is yours... the ship is yours — may it never sink."** The poet is praying to God to safeguard the light and pleading that the ship be kept from drowning. I used to like this song very much and hum it many times a day. Faith with the god is ok. After so much of trouble faced in the life, it felt like a sailing in the deep ocean. That's why I have written my autobiography entitled "The Arabian Sea: Magada's Expeditions of Life."

After this book, no matter what I tried to write, the sea would somehow seep into my words. Waves would curl between my sentences, the scent of salt would rise from the pages, and the whispers of the wind would nudge my thoughts back to the shore. Perhaps I had become entangled in the beauty of nature — not as an observer, but as a captive.

The more I tried to understand the tides, the clouds, the stillness before a storm, the more I realized that nature is not merely a backdrop to life — it is life. It shapes our moods, tests our endurance, and reminds us of our smallness in its vast scheme. In that process, I began to love life more deeply, but also more realistically. My faith shifted. Slowly, without bitterness, I became an atheist — not in denial of beauty, but in awe of it.

I stopped searching for god in temples and scriptures. Instead, I began to see god in the kindness of strangers, in the generosity of those who had little, in the quiet persistence of those who cared for life in all its forms. God became less of a being and more of a reflection — a mirror in which I saw compassion, courage, and truth.

One evening, as the sun dipped below the horizon and painted the ocean in molten gold, I felt an urge to speak to the god I no longer believed in — not to worship, but to converse. I took out a pen and paper, and wrote:

"Oh god, the lamp is mine... the wind is mine. The light will not fade. The ship is mine, the ocean is mine, and the ship will not drown."

It was not a plea. It was a declaration — a quiet assurance that the journey, with all its storms and still waters, was mine to navigate. The sea had taught me that more than speed, direction matters. And with my own compass — my gut, my hope, my love — I would sail on.

May be the unknown god was happy. He stopped bothering me; but the god began to observe me waiting me to fail. He/she thought I would call them again when I go to distress. More and more gods followed me. When I was surrounded with the so many curious gods, the odds in my road disappeared. Gods were jobless. I told them to be in the people I see, I love, I work with.

I light my own lamp, the wick was thicker, longer. I poured my divine energy which I got it from the hardship. I stood against the wind, so that light will glow forever..

As my friend a poet Mr. Asadullah Beg once said, *"I never changed the boat, I just changed the direction."* Those words stayed with me like a compass rose carved into the heart of a sailor. I did not abandon the vessel of my life; I merely turned the wheel. The moment I shifted my course, the lighthouse—once a distant myth—emerged from the haze, growing clearer with each measured mile.

I leaned over the side and gazed at the hull. Below the waterline, thousands of barnacles had fastened themselves like stubborn memories clinging to the skin of the past. Their white shells were like closed fists, guarding life within. Crabs scuttled over them, seeking a quick feast. When the danger drew near, the barnacles sealed themselves shut, not out of fear alone, but out of the ancient instinct to endure.

Some crabs fell back into the sea, tumbling into the deep. Yet many clawed their way up again, refusing to let go. It was a strange dance of survival—predator and prey bound together in an endless waltz. I wondered, are these creatures aware of the ship they ride on? Do they know they are moving across oceans, or do they believe the current itself is their doing?

Barnacles grip so tightly that when engineers scrape them off, the effort is immense—both in labour and in cost. Perhaps that is why old habits and attachments are so hard to shed: they fuse themselves to you, becoming part of your body until separation feels like injury.

Above, the air was alive with wings. Seagulls circled my ship, their cries sharp as salt in a wound. Were they following me because they had chosen my company, or were they using my course to find their own way home? Did they even know where home was?

I could not help but wonder if they were like us—humans—who so often mistake movement for purpose, or proximity for belonging. Some of us circle others endlessly, believing we are on our own journey, only to find we have been tethered to someone else's wake.

And so the sea kept teaching me, wave by wave: in life, as at sea, direction is everything. The speed matters little if your compass is wrong. And sometimes, what you think is pursuit is only drifting.

As the lighthouse drew closer, its beam cut through the horizon in rhythmic intervals — a pulse of hope, a reminder that even in the vast, indifferent ocean, there was a fixed point, unmoved by the waves and tempests. I began to wonder — was the lighthouse built to guide ships to shore, or was it also to remind sailors that they were not lost?

From afar, the beam seemed steady and serene. But as I drew nearer, I realized the lighthouse itself was weather-